Adventures in Toy-Making

Adventures in TOY-MAKING

Gillian Bradshaw-Smith

Illustrated with drawings by the author
and with photographs by Bob Hanson

Taplinger Publishing Company / New York

Second Printing

Published in the United States in 1976 by
TAPLINGER PUBLISHING CO., INC.
New York, New York

Library of Congress Catalog Card Number: 75-903

ISBN 0-8008-0102-4 (cloth)
ISBN 0-8008-0103-2 (paper)

Designed by Ellen Hsiao

Contents

Illustrations in Color

Foreword

To me the pleasure in making soft toys is as much if not more fun than the delight in the final results. First there is choosing the fabrics and colors and combining textures and colors—fur fabrics with silk, cotton with tweed, bright colors with soft, and deciding whether to use natural colors for an animal or whether to be outrageously fanciful.

Then there is the sheer pleasure in the actual making of the toy. Do give yourself plenty of time so you can enjoy it as the toy takes shape. It is so pleasant nowadays to make a toy in a thoughtful, gentle way and not just think, how fast can I get this bunny together? So give yourself time to relish the making of every toy you do. Then your final achievement won't be marred by any hasty work or abrupt decisions.

Finally there is the satisfaction in doing the finishing touches—the careful placement of whiskers or pupils of an eye. And what you decide to add or what to leave off. Here you can let your imagination go on the little details. My suggestions for finishing touches are suggestions only. You might want entirely different faces on the pretzel people—the faces I give in the book just happened to be the way I made them this time. But when you experiment with various finishing touches, pin or baste them in place. Pen and pencil marks have a nasty way of getting in the wrong place.

I like to keep the shapes of the toys I design as simple as possible and still create the effect I'm looking for which is a sense of liveliness, cuddliness, and charm. The sense of touch is very much involved in my concept of these toys. They should feel good, and be soft and cuddly. That is why in the directions I stress so much how they should be stuffed.

And finally I want to thank all the people at Possum Trot Corporation who have worked with me in seeing many of these designs come alive.

Gillian Bradshaw-Smith

Before You Start

If you have not made stuffed toys before, you may find working inside out a little confusing at first. You will almost always be working on the wrong side of the fabric. And so you should always remember when putting paws, ears, and tails into seams and slits that they should point in the right direction *when* the animal is turned right side out. It will seem like working backward until you get used to it. I've shaded the right side of the fabric in the drawings so you will know where you are at. There is a detailed drawing for almost every step which will show you what the toy will look like at that stage. Do check the drawing before you sew.

Sewing these toys is not difficult. Wherever there is a tricky part, I've mentioned it in the instructions as a warning to slow down and move carefully.

Drawing the Patterns

The patterns in this book, except for some of the smaller animals, are on grids. When there is no grid, you can simply trace the pattern on very thin bond or other slightly transparent paper since they are the exact size.

When the pattern is on a grid, it is quite easy to enlarge it by transferring it to a larger grid. The dimensions for drawing your own grid are given with each set of patterns. If you follow this scale, the toys will be the same size as those in the photographs in this book. Some of the animals look wonderful when they are enlarged even more. The elephant, the honey bear, the dolphin, and the seal are all splendid in a larger size. If you want to enlarge them, just increase the scale of the grid you draw.

To make your grid, use a large sheet of wrapping paper and rule parallel lines across and down according to the instructions for each pattern. Or you can draw them on graph paper. For some of the larger animals like the octopus, you will need a yardstick to draw the lines. You may wish to number the lines across and down so you will always know which square you are drawing in.

There are two simple techniques that make transferring the patterns from the book to your grid easier. First, notice where the line of the pattern intersects each line of the grid.

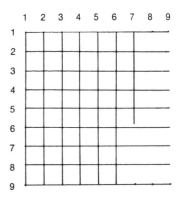

You can make a dot at that point. Second, notice the shapes the line of the pattern leaves on each side of the square. I have shaded part of one square in the drawings to show what I mean.

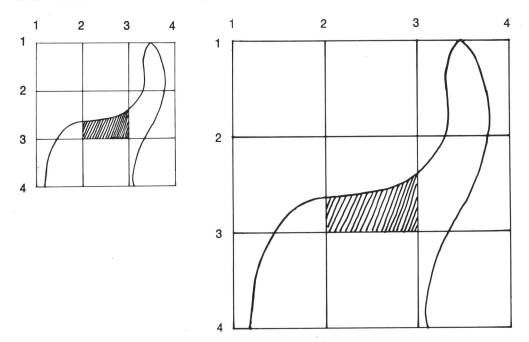

If you have never drawn from a grid before, it may take a couple of experiments to get the hang of it. Choose one of the simpler shapes for your first try and use a pencil so you can erase mistakes. You will be surprised how quickly you will be able to manage complicated shapes. And if you are one of those people who think you "can't draw a line," you may be more successful than some people who can draw, for they have a tendency to go off on their own.

If you wish to avoid using a grid, you can take the book to a photostating firm and have the pattern enlarged to the size you wish. It is not too costly a process, particularly if you ask for the negatives only, which are just as useful for making patterns as the positives.

When you cut your paper patterns, cut on the line you have drawn as the seam allowance is included in the pattern. Indicate all the letters on the patterns with marks, draw the ear slits and the darts, mark the dots for the eyes, and draw the arrows that indicate the way the nap runs.

When you are cutting a paper pattern that is symmetrical, such as the honey bear's ear, fold the paper pattern in half and cut both sides at once. In this way the two halves of the pattern will be identical.

Laying Out and Cutting

Lay out the fabric on a flat surface with the right side down. Arrange your patterns on the fabric, following the arrows that indicate the directions of the nap. I've found it helpful to draw an arrow on the selvage as it serves as a constant reminder.

If you are using fur fabric, velvet, or any fabric except smooth cotton or silk, don't fold it since it is hard to cut a double thickness accurately. Instead, draw around the pattern of one side on a single layer of fabric, then to reverse the other side, just flip the pattern over before you draw it. Also, it is best not to pin your paper patterns in place if you are using fur fabric or a bulky material. I find that weighing them down before cutting (a professional trick) is much more accurate.

It is easier to cut smooth cotton or silk in double layers. Fold your material with right sides facing. When you lay out your patterns, follow the arrows for the nap even if it is a solid color so the grain will run in the right direction. Before cutting, remove the paper pattern and pin the two layers of fabric together in the middle of each pattern piece to hold them in place before you cut around the pattern line.

A fine felt-tip pen is excellent for drawing the patterns on the fabric. On very dark fabrics use a tailor's chalk. When you draw the patterns also mark the As and Bs, etc., either by making tiny marks with a felt-tip pen or by cutting a tiny snip on the edge of the piece instead of notches. Mark the darts and the ear slits. The easiest way to mark the ear slits is to cut the slit in the paper pattern and then mark the fabric with a felt-point pen through the slit in the paper. When you cut the slit in the fabric, start in the middle and work to both ends but don't make the slit too long. It can always be lengthened.

After you have marked the eye dots and the piece has been

cut, pull a knotted, contrasting colored thread through the eye mark so it will show on the right side of the fabric as the eyes are put on after the toy has been turned and stuffed. The one time you shouldn't draw your patterns or marks is when you are making unlined felt ears, paws, and tails such as for the bush baby or the prairie dog since the marks will show on the finished toy. Instead, cut a piece of felt a little larger than the pattern, hold the paper pattern against it with your thumb and forefinger and cut around the paper pattern. Simple shapes of felt, such as small ears, can be cut two at a time and then they will be identical. If you are using thin felt, it is a good idea to give it the window test before you cut your pieces. Hold the felt up against a window to see if there are any weak spots and avoid them when you lay out your patterns.

Pattern Markings

The eyes are marked with a dot, slits are marked by a line with two small crossbars at the ends, and darts are marked with a diamond or narrow oval shape. The arrows indicate the direction of the nap or grain of the fabric. Letters identify corners and key points on the edges. The latter are marked with a small inked-in triangle.

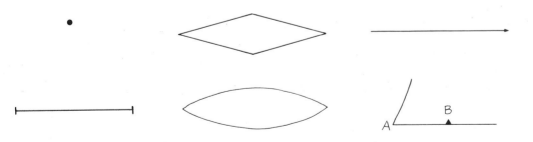

Working with Fur Fabrics

Fur fabrics come in a great variety of different thicknesses and lengths of pile, but they all have a knitted backing so they tend to be stretchy. This stretchiness is not difficult to cope with though it does require a little extra care. On the other hand when you have finished a toy in fur fabric, you will find that the pile hides a multitude of sins.

When you are reversing a side body pattern to make a right side and a left side or cutting any body piece, be very sure that the arrow is aligned exactly with the grain of the fabric. Even a slight tilt could make the matching curves stretch differently when you sew a side body piece to an underbody. This can be cured by easing as you pin and baste, but it is far simpler if the pieces are cut properly in the first place.

Sharp scissors are a pleasure to use and make cutting much easier. If the pile of the fabric is very thick or long, slide the scissors through it and try to cut only the backing of the cloth. The pile will separate as you pull the pieces apart. Cut the ear slits when you are ready to put the ears in. Otherwise the fabric around the slit may pull out of shape while you are putting the toy together.

Before you sew be very generous with your pinning. As you are working with the right sides of the fabric facing, you will find fur fabric slips and slides just like velvet. So pin and baste frequently. Pin a seam at the ends first, then at the middle, and then between so the curves will match exactly.

Use a heavier sewing machine needle for fur fabrics than you would for normal sewing. Use a longer stitch for the heavier fur fabrics. As you sew, push the fur back from the seam so as little as possible gets trapped in the stitches. Don't worry if some is caught, for a gentle brushing on the seams after a toy is finished will free it.

When you sew cotton or felt pieces—such as the octopus's tentacles or the monkey's face—to fur fabric, the bulk of the pile will make the cotton or felt piece seem a little skimpy. Just ease the cotton or felt on and pin and baste before you sew. Frequent pinning and basting is the secret when working with fur fabrics.

If you have never worked with fur fabric before, it is a good idea to practice with some scraps left over from your cutting. Try sewing some pieces with curves as well as straight seams. Practice keeping the seams at $\frac{3}{16}$ of an inch (5 mm) as well as ¼ of an inch (6 mm). Sew some angles. When you sew a sharp turn, keep the needle in the fabric, raise the presser foot, pivot the fabric on the needle, lower the presser foot, and continue in the new direction. Also practice sewing through several layers of fabric at the seam edges as though you were sewing in an ear or a tail. Slow the machine down as you approach the extra layers. If your machine cannot take these thicknesses of fur fabric, you can always backstitch these places firmly by hand.

Turning

Before you turn the toy right side out, check all the seams to see that there are no missing stitches. This is particularly important where three pieces of fabric meet, such as an underbody and two side pieces. If there are any missing stitches, you can run that part of the seam through the sewing machine again or backstitch firmly by hand. These toys and most of all the beanbag toys take quite a buffeting.

For a smoothly turned toy, the tension of the fabric on the seams should be released on the curves, points, and inner angles. Clip the outer curves by taking out small wedges close to the seam but not so close as to weaken it. On the inner curves just clip, and again not too close to the seam. Cut across the points, such as the tips of the dolphin's tail and up close to the seam on the inner angles, such as between the tentacles of the octopus or under the arms of the pretzel people.

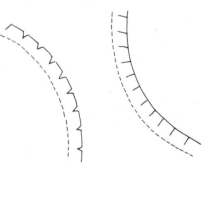

When you turn the toys right side out, work from the farthest extremities, gently poking in the thumb, then the hand, for example. Use the blunt end of a knitting needle or a dowel for such hard-to-reach spots as the octopus's tentacles. Poke all the limbs into the body and then start to pull them out of the opening, turning the body right side out last of all. It is very exciting to see the toy unfold like a butterfly from his inside-out cocoon. After he is turned, give him a shake, then check to see that all the little ends are turned completely. It is very annoying to have a toy half stuffed only to discover that a thumb or a toe is folded in. Use an orange stick, a crochet hook, or the blunt end of a knitting needle or a dowel to turn every last bit completely.

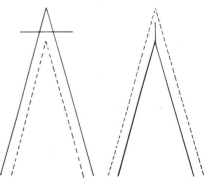

Stuffing

Stuffing has a lot to do with creating the form of the toy, and if it is done really well, it makes all the difference between a well-made, handsome toy and a lumpy or limp one. After you have turned the toy, it is a temptation to throw the stuffing in as fast as possible to see how the completed toy will look. If you are so tempted, it might be a good idea to put it aside for a while.

Stuffing a toy should be a leisurely and pleasurable process since it takes time to do it well. Before starting, check all the tips of the toes, bills, noses, and thumbs to see that they are completely turned. Then using small pieces of filling, push them gently into farthest parts—the nose and the legs— tamping them down with a dowel or the blunt end of a thick knitting needle. Build the stuffing evenly as you work up to the middle of the body. The key points are where the legs and the neck join the body. These should be filled completely and firmly so heads won't sag and legs won't wobble.

Stuffing isn't an automatic process. You can gain a great deal of pleasure in molding the toy as you stuff it. The flat- ness of the dolphin's jaw, the bridge of the monkey's nose which has so much to do with his expression, the calves of the rainbow dolls—all should be shaped as you work. So put aside time and enjoy stuffing. You will be rewarded with a nice, plump, smooth toy with character.

The quantities of stuffing material which I have given for the larger toys are only approximate as it is very much a personal choice as to how hard or how soft a toy may be made. And I've somewhat overestimated the amounts so you won't be caught short.

Beanbag fillings give an exciting feel and life to some of the smaller animals. And little children love them. Lentils or rice make excellent fillings, and the toys should be filled about three-quarters full. Be sure when you use a beanbag filling that the seams are thoroughly secure before you turn the toy right side out. I like to machine-zigzag stitch the raw edges. And if by any chance the seam is too close to the raw edge, I resew it.

Closing the Opening

When you close the opening, have some stuffing material handy as sometimes you will need to add a little extra as you work. Try to match the color of the thread to the fabric and use two strands of regular sewing thread. Buttonhole thread is also good for stitching fur fabric though it is too thick to use with other materials. Make a knot in the thread and secure it on the inside of the right-hand side of the opening and with tiny overcast stitches gradually work the opening closed, folding the raw edges in as you go.

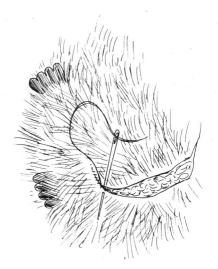

Add filling if you need it to keep the last part of the toy as pleasantly plump as the rest. Continue overcasting and firming up the stuffing, if the toy needs it, until the opening is closed. Make sure you finish off the thread very securely as closing must stay closed.

A Note About the Illustrations

Since all these toys are made wrong side out with the right sides of the fabric facing except for a few details, I have shaded the right side of the fabric in the drawings and left the wrong side unshaded. I hope this will serve as a helpful reminder as you put the toys together.

When an ear, tail, or fin is to be sewn into a seam, I have drawn the ⅛ of an inch (3 mm) of the base which should project. And when the tail or paw is folded, I've indicated which way the fold should face. I have also used a dotted line to indicate its position when you cannot see it through the fabric.

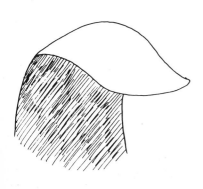

I have used the usual symbols for pinning, basting, and sewing.

I've drawn the contrasting colored thread pulled through to the right side of the fabric to mark the eyes. On the wrong side, it is represented by a knot.

I have also drawn small notches to mark the lettered points where you will be cutting tiny slits or marking with a felt-tip pen, but the notches are easier to follow.

Note on Measurements

The metric equivalents of inches are given in parentheses. To make measuring simpler, the metric figure is not necessarily an accurate conversion, but it is the better round number for the particular purpose for which it is being used.

No conversion is given for transferring the patterns onto squared grids, as the fractional differences in the metric conversion would alter the patterns.

Bush Baby

The bush baby is an enchanting little animal from the rain forests of Africa with enormous eyes and soft fur. Bush babies make fine toys for very young children as the big eyes are most effective when they are made of fabric and then there are no buttons to chew off. And the long tails are great for small children to play with.

It seems to me that they are best made in a fairly realistic way with a fluffy fur fabric of golden brown or yellow ocher or beige. The ears can be left unlined or lined with fine cotton or silk. I made the eyes of this one in amber satin with black felt pupils.

They are easy toys to make. The pattern has only a few pieces and the tail looks best handsewn and the overcasting goes quickly as the stitches will be hidden in the pile. As the bush baby is really just a small ball of fur (he is only six inches tall not counting his tail), it is worthwhile to take care in the little details such as the felt feet.

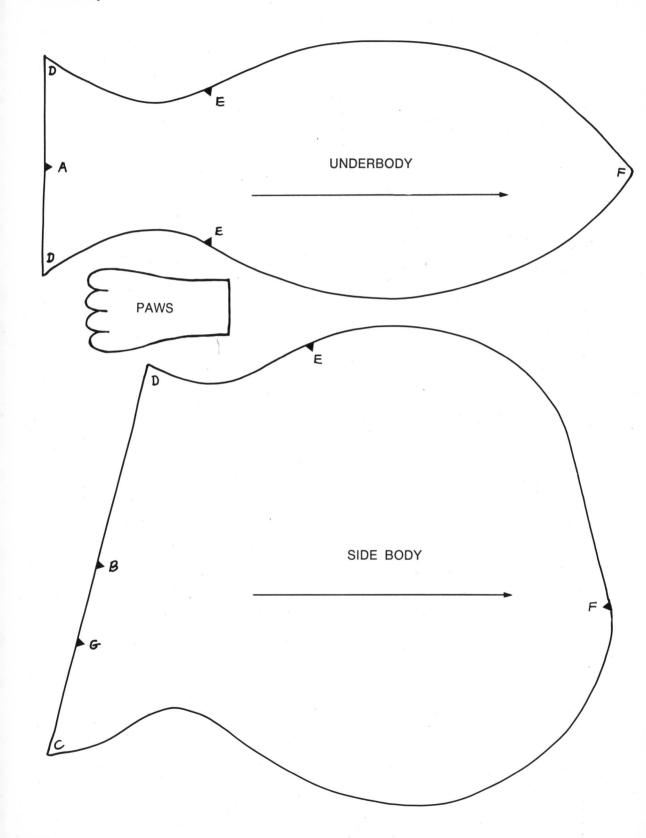

D

E

A

UNDERBODY

F

D

E

PAWS

E

D

B

SIDE BODY

F

G

C

You will need

- Fur fabric for body, 18 inches by 10 inches
  (46 cm by 25 cm)
- Felt for paws and tongue, a scrap
- Satin or other material for the eyes, a scrap
- Thin cotton or silk for ear lining, a scrap
- Dacron polyester or old nylon stockings cut up fine for
  stuffing, or a beanbag filling (rice or lentils)

The patterns for the bush baby are the exact size, so they can
be traced. There is no pattern for the tail as it is cut by meas-
urement.

Cutting

Lay out the fur fabric wrong side up and place your patterns
on it, following the directions of the arrows so the nap runs
from head to tail. Begin by cutting 2 side body pieces, flipping
the pattern over when you cut the second so that you will
have a right and a left side. Cut 1 underbody, 1 face, and 2
ears. Cut the tail by measuring a length of fabric 1½ inches
by 16 inches (38 mm by 41 cm), making sure to cut it with the
nap running lengthwise.

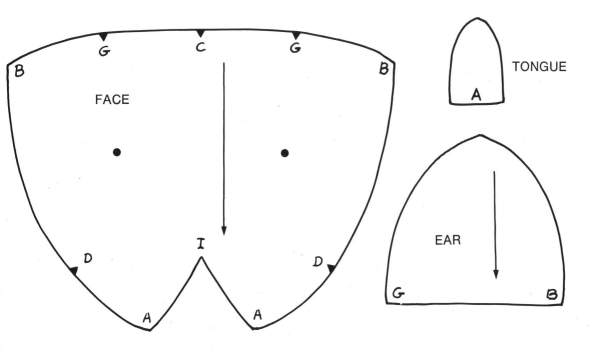

When you cut the felt paws and tongue, do not draw around the patterns since the marks will not be hidden by seams and would show on the finished animal. Simply hold the pattern firmly against the felt with your thumb and forefinger and cut around the pattern. Cut 4 paws and 1 tongue.

If you are planning to line the ears, cut 2 ears of the lining material.

Mark the As, Bs, etc. Pull a knotted thread of contrasting color through to the right side of the fabric of the face piece to mark the eyes.

Sewing

All seams should be ⅜₆ of an inch (5 mm).

If you are lining the ears, sew the ear linings in, right sides of the fabrics facing, around the edge of the ear, leaving the base of the ear unsewn for turning. Clip the seams at the curves and turn right side out.

Step 1. Fold the tail lengthwise with the right side of the fabric outside and the nap running from the base to the tip of the tail. Overcast by hand, using as small stitches as possible, and be sure to sew the tip closed.

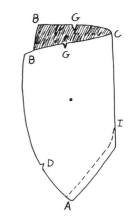

Step 2. Fold the face from C to I with the right sides of the fabric facing. Match the As and sew up dart from A to I, tapering the seam when you reach the fold.

Step 3. Fold a paw lengthwise and tack on the right side of the fabric of one of the body pieces at E with the fold toward D and the paw pointing in toward the body. Leave ⅛ of an inch (3mm) of the base of the paw showing on the wrong side of the fabric so it will be caught securely in the seam. Pin and sew the side body piece to the underbody piece from F to D, sewing the wrist of the paw into the seam at the same time.

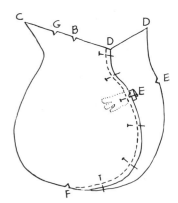

Step 4. Before sewing the second body piece to the underbody, tack the base of the tail on the right side of the fabric just above F with the tail folded into the inside of the body and ⅛ of an inch (3 mm) showing from the wrong side of the fabric. Tack the other front paw at E as in step 3. Then pin and sew from D to 2½ inches (64 mm) above F, leaving an opening for turning and stuffing. Continue from F, sewing the base of the tail firmly in place, and on up to C.

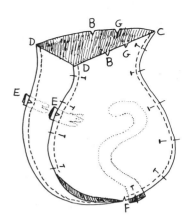

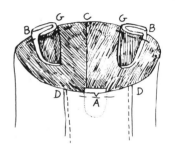

Step 5. Fold the ears in half lengthwise with the wrong side of the fabric (or the lining) on the inside and baste onto the right side of the fabric of the side body pieces between the Bs and Gs, with the folds of the ears toward C and ⅛ of an inch (3 mm) showing from the wrong side of the fabric. Tack the tongue onto the right side of the underbody fabric, centering it at A with ⅛ of an inch (3 mm) showing above the underbody.

Step 6. Pin the face, wrong side of the fabric up, to the body, matching the As at the center front, the Cs at the center back, and the Bs and the Gs. Then pin and sew right around the face.

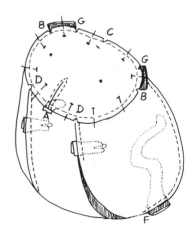

Turning and Stuffing

Clip the curves of the face and check all the seams, particularly where three places meet, to see if there are any missing stitches which should be resewn. Turn right side out and stuff. If you are using a beanbag filling, fill only three-quarters full. If you are stuffing the bush baby with Dacron polyester or old nylon stockings, the stuffing should be medium soft. You will quickly get the knack of stuffing these toys so that you can tell by the feel of the animal when he is just right. Close the opening with a small overcast stitch.

Finishing

Brush the seams gently to free any hair that has been caught in the stitching.

To make the fabric eyes, see page 124. I made the fabric eyes on this bush baby of 1¾-inch (44-mm) circles of satin and glued on 1-inch (25-mm) felt pupils. I like to center the pupils as this gives him an appealing air of surprise.

Sew the back paws into position so you can just see the toes when the bush baby is sitting down. Anchor them firmly at the wrists with a small overcast stitch.

Mole

Moles are very velvety in real life so I think velvet in a nice dark brown, dark gray, or black with pale pink nose and paws is very attractive. But he is equally handsome in plush or a short fur fabric. If you do make him in velvet or velveteen, remember that they are slippery fabrics to work with so be generous with the pins before you sew the seams.

He is very easy to make as he has no ears or tail. There is only one dart in the underbody which gives him a little additional shape. The mole is only six and a half inches long so he makes an ideal beanbag toy. Or he can be stuffed with a soft filling.

You will need

- Body fabric, 14 inches by 9 inches (36 cm by 23 cm)
- Felt for nose and paws, 8 inches by 2 inches (21 cm by 5 cm)
- 2 beads for eyes, ¼ of an inch in diameter (6 mm) (optional)
- Embroidery thread for eyes (optional)
- Beanbag filling (rice or lentils) or Dacron polyester or old nylon stockings cut up fine for stuffing

The patterns for the mole are the exact size so they can be traced to make your paper patterns.

Cutting

Lay out the body fabric wrong side up and place your pattern pieces on it, following the directions of the arrows so the nap runs from the nose at A to B at the tail. Cut 2 side body pieces. When you cut the second, reverse the pattern by flipping it over so there will be a left side and a right side. Cut 1 under-body piece.

Mark the As, Bs, etc., and the dart in the underbody piece. Mark the dot for the eye by pulling a knotted, contrasting colored thread through to the right side of the fabric.

Cut 2 noses and 4 paws from the felt. Do not draw around the paw pattern on the felt since the marks will not be hidden by seams and would show. Just hold the pattern firmly against the felt with your thumb and forefinger and cut around the pattern carefully.

The curving claws of the paws are very delicate and are best cut by eye. The surest way to do this is first to cut a curving line down the middle and then cut another curving line down the middle of each half. Then shape the four claws one at a time.

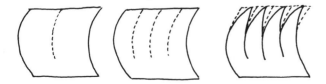

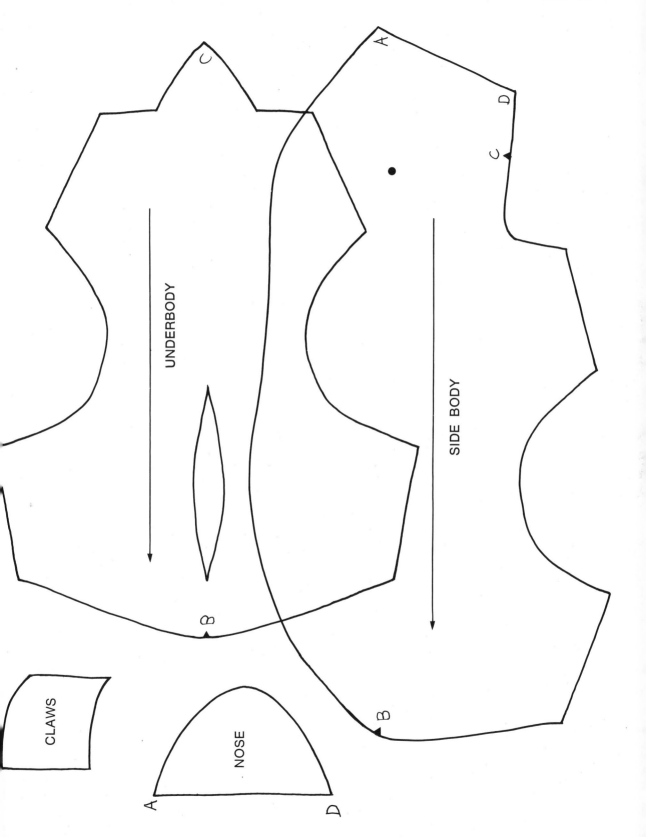

UNDERBODY

SIDE BODY

CLAWS

NOSE

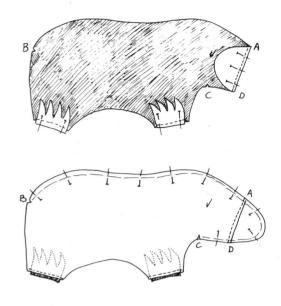

Sewing

All seams should be ³⁄₁₆ of an inch (5 mm).

Step 1. Pin and sew a nose piece to the right side of the fabric of a side body piece from A to D as in the sketch. Then place two paws at the bottoms of the legs with the claws curving back toward B. Pin and sew them on, following the sketch. Repeat with the other side body piece.

Step 2. With the right sides of the fabric facing, pin and baste the two side body pieces together from C around the nose and down the back to B. Be careful to see that the seams of the felt nose between A and D match exactly.

Step 3. Sew the dart in the underbody piece and cut away excess material. Pin and baste the underbody to one side of the sewn body section, right sides of the fabric facing, from B to C up one side. Repeat on the other side, but leave an opening of 2½ inches (64 mm) between the legs for turning and stuffing. Sew from C through B and back to C again except for the opening, making sure that the claws are not caught in the seams.

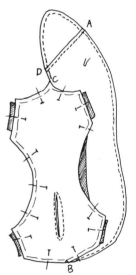

Turning and Stuffing

Clip the curves and check all the seams, particularly at C and B, to see if they are properly sewn, and resew any places where there are any missing stitches. If you have used a fabric that frays easily such as velvet, machine-zigzag or hand-whip the raw edges.

Turn right side out and stuff. If you are using a beanbag filling, fill about three-quarters full. If you are using Dacron polyester or nylon stocking pieces, stuff fairly soft.

Finishing

The eyes can be satin-stitched with embroidery thread. If you wish to use small beads, see page 126.

Prairie Dog

This upright little animal makes a fine, fluffy beanbag for a child. He feels good to touch and to stroke, and I find adults like him too. For a very young infant he should be stuffed.

The pattern pieces are so small (he is only five inches high), and he can be made in so many different colors and textures of fur fabric, that this is a good way to use up small pieces of fabric left over from a larger toy. And he is simple to make. His tail, for instance, is unlined and unsewn and cut from one thickness of fur fabric.

When I make him, I like to keep the colors of the felt ears and paws, and the thread whiskers and stem-stitched mouth coordinated with the body fabric so they don't stand out too much. But that's because I think of him as a rather shy animal. You may want to make him in more startling colors.

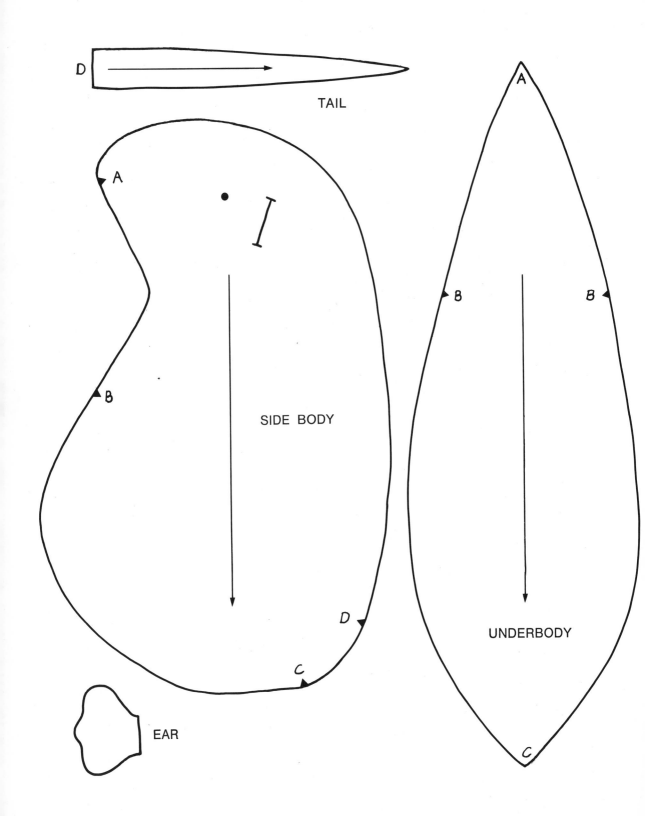

TAIL

SIDE BODY

UNDERBODY

EAR

You will need

- Body fabric, 12 inches by 12 inches (31 cm by 31 cm)
- Felt for paws and ears, a scrap
- 2 flat buttons, ⅜ of an inch (9 mm) in diameter, for eyes (optional)
- Embroidery thread for the mouth and nose
- Beanbag filling (rice or lentils) or Dacron polyester or old nylon stockings cut up fine for stuffing

The patterns for the prairie dog are the exact size so they can be traced. Use the white mice pattern on page 34 for the paws. And follow the directions for cutting them on page 35.

Cutting

Lay out fur fabric wrong side up and place your pattern pieces on it, following the directions of the arrows so the nap runs from head to tail. Cut 2 side bodies, flipping the pattern over to reverse the second so that you will have a right and a left side. Cut 1 underbody and 1 tail.

Cut 2 ears and 4 paws from the felt. Do not draw around the ear and paw patterns since the marks will not be hidden by seams and would show. Just hold the pattern firmly against the felt with your thumb and forefinger and cut around the pattern carefully.

Mark the As, Bs, etc., and the ear slits. Pull a knotted thread of contrasting color through to the right side of the fabric to mark the eyes.

Sewing

All seams should be 3/16 of an inch (5 mm).

Step 1. Cut the ear slits in the side body pieces. Push the base of the ears through the ear slits from the right side of the fabric. ⅛ of an inch (3 mm) of the base should show on the wrong side of the fabric so the ear will be sewn into the seam securely. Pinch the slit together and, working on the wrong side of the fabric, sew down catching both sides firmly.

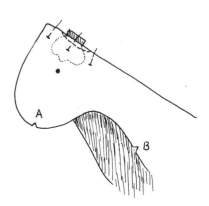

Step 2. Fold one paw lengthwise and tack at B of one side body piece with the fold facing up toward the head and the paw pointing in toward the body with ⅛ of an inch (3 mm) showing from the wrong side of the fabric. Then pin and sew the side body piece to the underbody, starting at A at the nose and continuing toward C, sewing the wrist of the paw firmly into the seam. Leave an opening of approximately 2½ inches (64 mm) before C for turning and stuffing.

Step 3. Before sewing the second side body to the underbody, tack the second folded paw in place at B as you did the first. Fold the tail lengthwise and tack it with the fold up just below D with ⅛ of an inch (3 mm) showing from the wrong side of the fabric. Then pin and sew from A through B over the wrist of the paw to C. Continue around the back, sewing the base of the tail in firmly, and up to A.

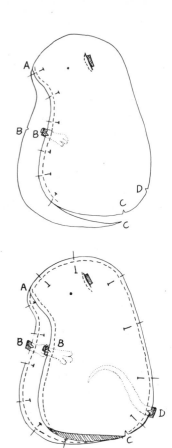

Turning and Stuffing

Clip all curves and check all the seams, particularly at the nose where three pieces of fabric meet. If stitches are not sewn tightly or there are any stitches missing, reinforce by hand. Then turn right side out.

If you are planning to use the prairie dog as a beanbag, fill him only three-quarters full. If you are using Dacron polyester or stocking pieces, leave the stuffing soft. Close the opening with a small overcast stitch.

Finishing

Sew the button eyes on (see page 126). Or if the prairie dog is for a younger child, embroider them with embroidery thread in a satin stitch or glue on small rounds of felt.

Embroider the nose with a satin stitch with embroidery thread. Use the same thread for the lines of the mouth, using a stem stitch (see page 128). For the whiskers, see page 127.

Place the hind paws on the underbody so the toes will just show when the prairie dog sits up and sew them down firmly at the ankles with an overcast stitch.

The bush baby and the
seal are easy to make
and adults as well as
children love them.

Occasionally I like to mix the large and the small for a gift.

White Mice

These white mice are very dainty and delicate. They have little pink paws, pink noses, pink ears, and pink eyes and tails. They look very real in white but they also look charming in beige, creamy brown, or gray.

I made them out of a lightweight, short-piled white fur fabric since you cannot work on such a small scale—they stand only four inches high—with very heavy pile. You can also use a brushed flannel, velvet or velveteen, felt or fine wool, but the ears, tail, and feet should be felt. You can embroider the nose or make one of felt.

I always like to make them in pairs as they are such gregarious little creatures. They are not quite so easy to make as the prairie dog and the mole because they have more subtle contours and the sewing must be accurate. Nevertheless they are not difficult, and the actual sewing time is very short.

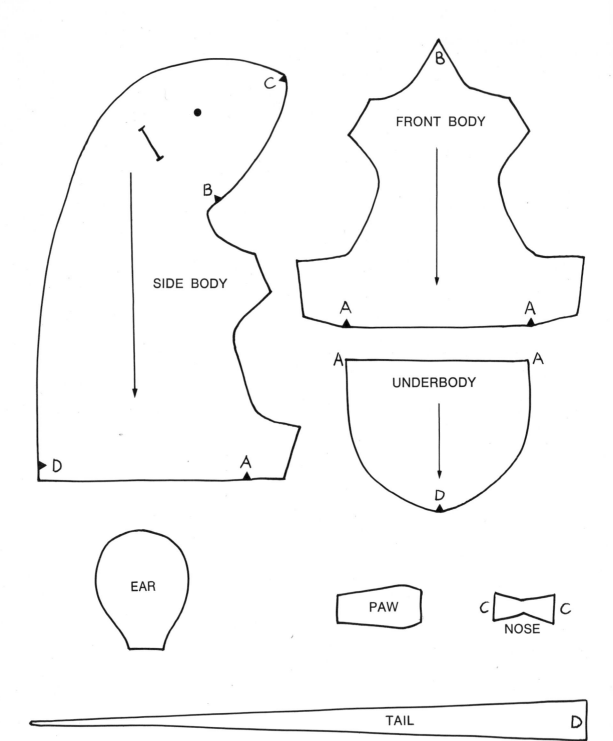

SIDE BODY

FRONT BODY

UNDERBODY

EAR

PAW

NOSE

TAIL

You will need for one mouse
- Fabric for body, 8 inches by 6 inches (21 cm by 15 cm)
- Felt for tail, ears, nose, and paws, 6 inches by 2 inches (15 cm by 51 mm)
- Embroidery thread for nose and eyes (optional)
- 2 beads for eyes, ⅛ of an inch (3 mm) in diameter (optional)
- Dacron polyester or old nylon stockings for stuffing

The patterns for the white mice are the exact size so they can be traced to make your paper patterns.

Cutting
Lay out the body fabric wrong side up. Place your patterns on it, following the directions of the arrows so the nap runs from the nose to the tail. Cut 1 underbody and 1 front body. Cut 2 side body pieces, and when you cut the second, flip the pattern over so there will be a right side and a left side.

Mark the As, Bs, etc., and the slits for the ears. Mark the dots for the eyes by pulling a knotted, contrasting colored thread through to the right side of the fabric.

Cut 1 nose, 2 ears, 1 tail, and 4 paws from the felt. Since these will have raw edges, do not mark with pen or pencil which would show. Just hold the pattern firmly against the felt with your thumb and forefinger and cut around it carefully.

The mouse's toes are very delicate and are best cut by eye. The easiest way to do this is first to cut a line down the middle and then cut another line down the middle of each half. Then shape the toes one at a time.

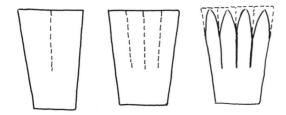

Sewing
All seams should be ³⁄₁₆ of an inch (5 mm).

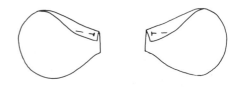

Step 1. Fold the ears by one-third so the top of the ear is curled and pin the fold in place. This gives the mouse an alert, inquisitive look.

Step 2. Cut the slits for the ears. With the fold toward the top of the head and the nose, poke the base of the ears through the slits from the right side of the fabric so ⅛ of an inch (3 mm) shows on the wrong side. Pin and sew on the wrong side, catching the fabric of the head firm-ly on each side of the ear.

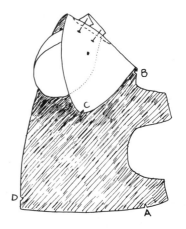

Step 3. Fold the tail in half at the wide end and tack on the right side of the fabric just above D on one of the side body pieces, with the fold toward the ears and the tail pointing in.

If you are using a felt nose, fold it in half and tack it on the right side of the fabric at C, with ¼ of an inch (6 mm) of the fold in from C.

Fold two paws in half and tack them to the right side of the fabric at the bottom of the legs with the folds toward B with ⅛ of an inch (3 mm) showing from the wrong side of the fabric. Be sure to have the toes pointing inward. Repeat with the other two paws on the other side body piece.

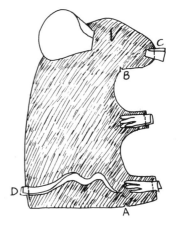

Step 4. Pin and sew the front body piece to one side body piece, matching the As and Bs, right sides of the fabric facing. Align the curves of the legs and sew right across the felt paws.

Step 5. Pin and sew the other side body piece to the front body piece and again sew right across the felt paws. Be sure to catch all three pieces of the fabric where they meet at B. From B continue to sew the two side body pieces together up the throat to C and over the top of the head, being careful not to catch the ears in the seam. Continue down the back to D, sewing in the base of the tail firmly.

Step 6. Pin the D of the underbody to the D of the body. Pin the As and then pin around, leaving a space between A and D on one side for turning and stuffing. Sew from D to A and then to the second A.

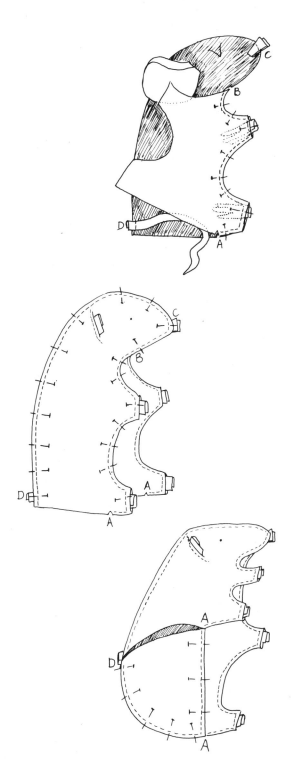

Turning and Stuffing

Check all the seams to see if they are properly sewn and clip the curves. When you turn the mouse right side out, don't tug on the paws too hard as they are delicate. Use an orange stick or a crochet hook to get every part completely turned.

Use very small pieces of Dacron polyester for the stuffing. For the nose and the legs, use pea-sized pieces and stuff them first. If you use old nylon stockings, cut them into small pieces. Flatten the bottom as you put in the last of the stuffing so your mouse will sit up perkily. Close the opening with small over-cast stitches.

Finishing

If you are embroidering the nose, a satin stitch is nice and shiny. If the mouse is for an older child, you may wish to use beads for eyes (see page 126). Or you can embroider the eyes with a satin stitch or glue on tiny rounds (⅛ of an inch [3mm] in diameter) of felt.

The whiskers should be done last. Single-strand embroidery thread makes fine whiskers for a mouse. For making whiskers, see page 127.

Baby Seal

For this baby seal I chose a pale gray fur fabric, but he is more realistic in a white or cream fabric as baby harp seals are creamy white when they are young. Or he can be done in a nice, rich brown or mottled fabric. You don't have to use a fur fabric; velvet, plush, or terry cloth are fine too.

He will come out fourteen inches long if you follow the grid instructions, but this is one of the toys that scales up very well and you can double his size if you wish. At fourteen inches long he makes a good beanbag toy. When I use a beanbag filling, I stuff his head and neck with Dacron polyester first so he will have that roundheaded seal quality.

His eyes are important. They should be domed buttons, not flat ones, to give him the inquiring look baby seals have.

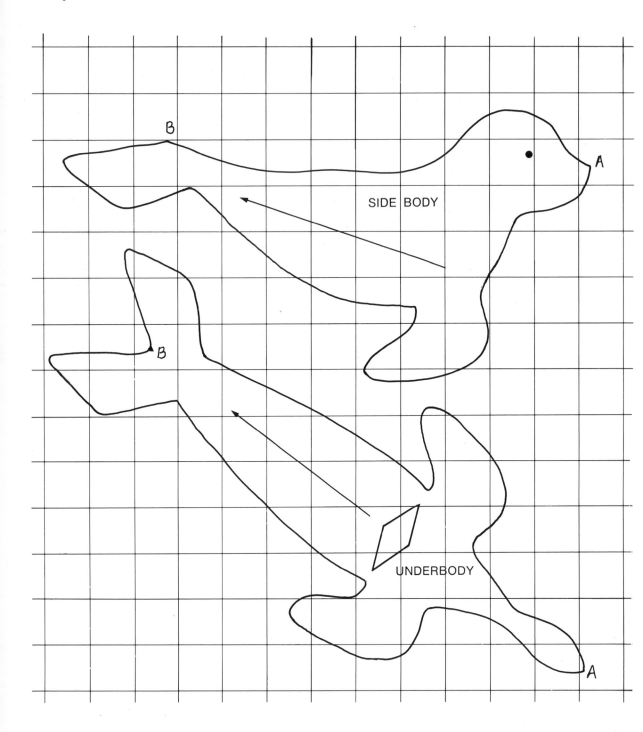

You will need

- Body fabric, 24 inches by 24 inches (61 cm by 61 cm)
- 2 round black buttons for eyes, ½ of an inch (13 mm) in diameter
- Buttonhole thread for whiskers
- Dacron polyester for stuffing, 4 ounces, or Dacron polyester and beanbag filling (lentils or rice)

To draw the patterns, rule lines on wrapping paper across and down 1½ inches apart to make 1½-inch by 1½-inch squares. Copy the pattern onto these squares (see page 10).

Cutting

Lay out the fabric wrong side up. Place your patterns on it, following the directions of the arrows so the nap runs from nose to tail. Cut 2 sides, flipping the pattern over to reverse the second. Cut 1 underbody. Mark the As and the Bs and the dart on the underbody. Mark the eyes by knotting a contrasting colored thread and pulling it through to the right side of the fabric.

Sewing

All the seams should be ¼ of an inch (6 mm).

Step 1. Pin and sew the two side body pieces together, right sides of the fabric facing, from A to B along the back. If you are working with velvet, it slips easily, so it is best to pin frequently and baste before you sew.

Step 2. Sew the dart in the underbody and cut away excess material. Then pin the underbody to one side of the top section. Pin at A, right sides of the fabric facing, and pin the front flipper tips and the back flipper tips together. Then pin, baste, and sew the entire seam up to B. No matter what fabric you are using, it is better to pin and baste the seam so the curves match exactly before you sew it.

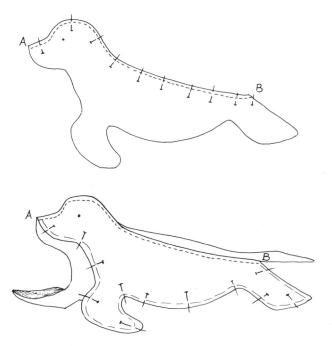

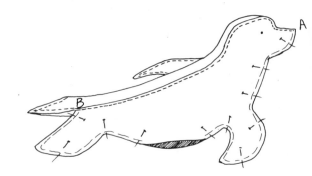

Step 3. Pin, baste, and sew the second under-body side to the other side of the top section, following the same procedure as in step 2. Leave an opening of around 3 inches (8 cm) between the flippers for turning and stuffing.

Turning and Stuffing

Clip the curves and cut across the ends of the points at the tips of the back flippers close to the seams. Check the seams to see if they need reinforcing by hand anywhere. If your seal is velvet or any fabric that frays easily, machine-zigzag the raw edges of the seams or overcast by hand.

When you turn the seal right side out, use the blunt end of a knitting needle or a crochet hook to turn the nose and the tips of the back flippers completely.

If you are using Dacron polyester for the stuffing, pull off small pieces for the nose, head, and neck and stuff them more firmly. Also stuff the front flippers a little more firmly than the rest of the body.

If you are using a beanbag filling, first stuff the head and the neck with Dacron polyester. Then follow with the beanbag filling, working it firmly into the ends of the flippers. Fill the rest of the body about three-quarters full, leaving enough space for the fill to shift around. Close the opening with small overcast stitches.

Finishing

For sewing on the button eyes, see page 126.
For sewing the whiskers, see page 127.

Mother Sheep and Lamb

This mother sheep with her lamb makes an impressive toy as she is eighteen inches long. And I've found that this pair appeals to grown-ups as much as to children.

I made the ones in the photograph in a yellowy-cream curled pile, an imitation lamb fabric. But I have also made them in a much smaller curled pile and in fur fabric too, and they came out beautifully. For the lower legs and the nose, I used a short-piled black fur fabric, but they can be done in plush, velvet, velveteen, or felt. You can give the mother sheep one lamb or two as there are two snaps on her udder. I once gave the mother a pair of lambs, one cream and the other black, and thought they made a fetching trio.

The little lamb, which is only eight inches long, is easy to make as his pattern is much simpler than the mother's. With a satin bow tied around his neck, he makes an enchanting gift all by himself.

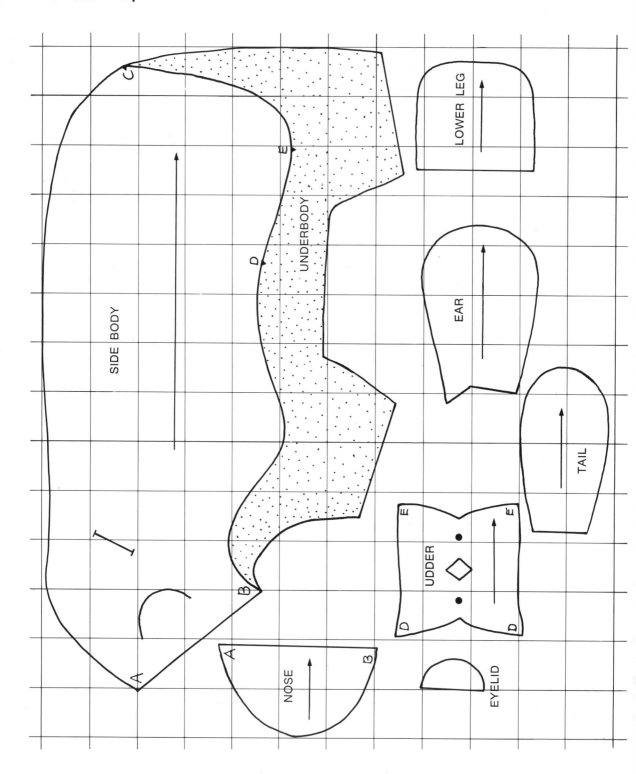

The Mother Sheep

You will need

- Body fabric, 27 inches by 40 inches (69 cm by 102 cm)
- Fabric for the lower legs and the nose, 18 inches by 12 inches (46 cm by 31 cm)
- Fine cotton or silk for lining the ears and the tail, scraps
- Embroidery wool for the eyelashes
- Glue for the eyelashes
- 2 positive snaps
- Dacron polyester for stuffing, nearly 2 pounds

To draw the patterns, rule lines on wrapping paper across and down 1½ inches apart to make 1½-inch by 1½-inch squares. Copy the patterns onto these squares (see page 10).

When you draw these patterns, it is important that the side body pattern and the underbody pattern match. There is a very easy way to do this. Draw around the entire outline of the side body pattern, including the polka-dotted area of the legs and the stomach. Then draw the curved line at the top of the polka-dotted area across your pattern.

Before you cut this pattern, place it over another sheet of paper and cut two identical patterns around the outside lines at the same time. Pay no attention to the curved line over the polka-dotted area at this time.

The paper pattern of the whole sheep without the drawn curved line over the polka-dotted area is your side body pattern. Then take the paper pattern with the curved line drawn on it and cut along the curve. Discard the upper portion and the lower half is your underbody pattern. You then have perfect matches which make sewing the seams much easier and will produce a well-tailored toy.

Cutting

Lay out the fabric for the body wrong side up. Place your patterns on it, following the directions of the arrows so the nap runs from the head to the tail. Cut 2 side body pieces, flipping the pattern over to reverse it for the second so there will be a right side and a left side. Cut 2 underbodies, reversing one. Cut 2 ears, reversing one. Cut 1 tail, 1 udder, and 2 eyelids. Lay out the fabric for the lower legs and nose wrong side up and again place the patterns with the arrows following the direction of the nap. Then cut 8 lower legs and 2 noses.

Cut 2 ears, reversing one, and 1 tail from the lining fabric.

Mark the As, Bs, etc., and the slits for the ears. Mark the curve of the eyelids with a running stitch in a contrasting colored thread, pulling it through to the right side of the fabric. Mark the two dots for the snaps on the udder by pulling a knotted thread of contrasting color through to the right side of the fabric.

Sewing
All seams should be ¼ of an inch (6 mm).

Step 1. Sew in the linings of the ears and the tail, right sides of the fabrics facing, leaving the bases open for turning. Clip the seams on the curves and turn right side out.

Step 2. Lay a nose piece on a side body piece, right sides of the fabrics facing, and pin and sew from A to B. Lay two lower leg pieces at the ends of the legs of the side body piece, right sides of the fabrics facing, and pin, baste, and sew across. Repeat with the other side body piece.

Step 3. Lay two lower leg pieces at the ends of the legs of an underbody piece, right sides of the fabrics facing, and pin and sew across. Repeat with the other underbody piece.

Step 4. Cut the diamond-shaped opening in the center of the udder. Sew two positive snaps on the right side of the fabric. Fold in half on the dotted line so the right sides of the fabric are facing. Pin and sew from D down to the fold and from E down to the fold, then pin and sew along the raw edges of the inverted V in the center. Clip the seams at the angles and turn right side out.

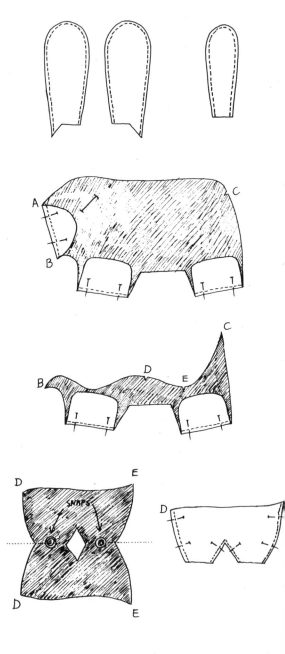

Step 5. Cut the ear slits in the side body pieces. Fold the ears as they are in the drawing which will give them a chipper look. Pin and baste the fold in place.

Step 6. Push the base of the ears through the slits from the right side of the fabric with the fold toward the top of the head and the lining facing toward the nose. ⅛ of an inch (3 mm) of the base of the ear should show from the wrong side of the fabric. Pinch the slit together and sew the base of the ear in firmly so both sides of the slit are caught together. If you are using a deep-piled fabric and have difficulty in machine-sewing it, backstitch firmly by hand.

Step 7. Baste the udder to the right side of the fabric of an underbody piece with the Ds and the Es matching and ⅛ of an inch (3 mm) of the top showing from the wrong side. Then put the two underbody pieces together, right sides of the fabric facing, matching the Bs at the throat and the Cs at the tail. Pin, baste, and sew from B to C. Again if you have difficulty in machine-sewing the udder into the seam, you can back-stitch it firmly by hand.

Step 8. Fold the tail lengthwise with the lining inside and baste it with the fold toward the top of the back just above C on the right side of the fabric of a side body piece. ⅛ of an inch (3 mm) of the base of the tail should show from the wrong side.

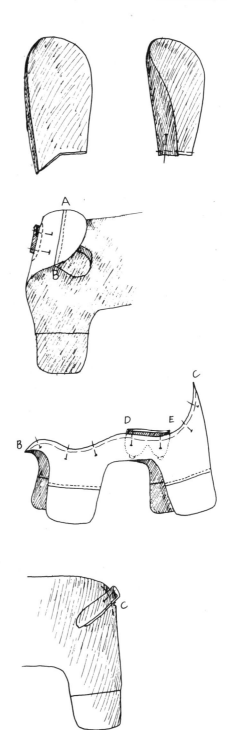

Step 9. Place the sewn underbody section on one side body piece, right sides of the fabric facing, matching the Bs and the Cs. Pin, baste, and sew the two together from B to C around the legs.

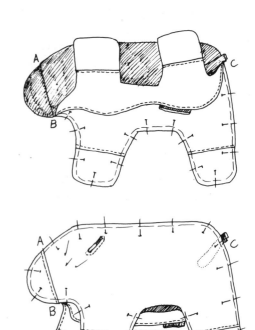

Step 10. Then sew on the other side body piece. Be careful to match the seams at the As and Bs on the nose exactly. Pin, baste, and sew from A around the nose to B and down the legs and up. Leave an opening of approximately 5 inches (13 cm) between the legs for turning and stuffing. Continue around the legs and up to C and along the top of the back to A. If machine-sewing the tail into the seam is difficult, it can be backstitched firmly by hand.

Turning and Stuffing

Clip on the curves and check the seams for any weak spots, particularly at B at the throat and at C at the tail. If any, reinforce with hand sewing. Turn right side out.

As the mother sheep is a standing toy, the legs and the places where the legs join the body should be stuffed very firmly. Also stuff the head and the neck firmly. Close the opening with small overcast stitches.

Finishing

Glue short lengths of wool embroidery thread on the wrong side of the eyelids to form eyelashes. Trim after the glue has dried.

Pin the eyelids in place, the right side of the fabric up, and sew them onto the head with small hemming stitches.

A barnyard scene with a mole and a prairie dog

The octopus and the
dolphin make fine
companions.

This silky, lemony,
long-piled fabric gives
a different look to
the usual teddy bear. So
he was rechristened
honey bear.

The Lamb

You will need for one lamb

- Body fabric, 14 inches by 11 inches (36 cm by 28 cm)
- Fine cotton or silk for lining ears and tail, a scrap
- Embroidery thread for eyes
- Dacron polyester for stuffing. If you are making a single lamb, old nylon stockings cut up fine can be used.

To draw the patterns, rule lines on wrapping paper across and down 1 inch apart to make 1-inch by 1-inch squares. Copy the patterns onto these squares (see page 10). Make the patterns for the side body pieces and the underbody pieces by the same method used for the mother sheep.

Cutting

Lay out the fabric wrong side up. Place your patterns on it, following the directions of the arrows so the nap runs from the nose to the tail. Cut 2 side bodies, reversing one, 2 underbodies, reversing one, and 2 ears of the body fabric and 2 ears of lining material. Cut 2 tails, 1 of body fabric and 1 of lining material.

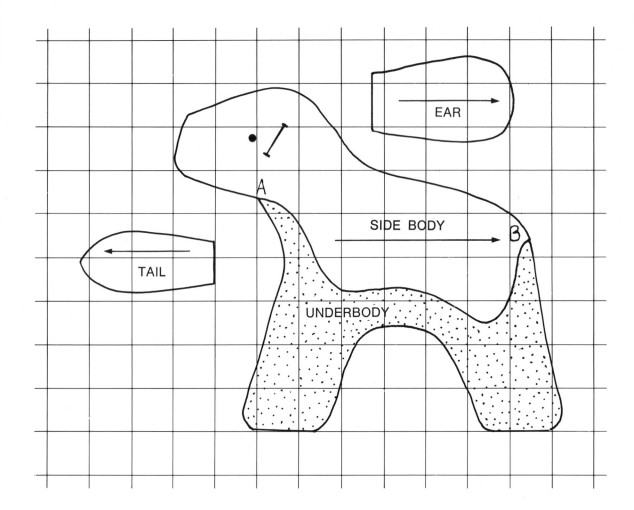

Mark the As and Bs and the ear slits. Mark the position of the eyes by pulling a knotted, contrasting colored thread through to the right side of the fabric.

Sewing

All seams should be ¼ of an inch (6 mm).

Line and turn the ears and the tail following the directions for the mother sheep. As the lamb's ears are much simpler, merely fold them in half lengthwise before you sew them in, making sure the fold is toward the top of the head. Baste the tail on at B as in the mother sheep. Pin, baste, and sew the two underbodies together, right sides of the fabric facing, from A to B as in the mother sheep.

Step 1. Pin, baste, and sew the sewn underbody section to one side body, right sides of the fabric facing, from A around the legs to B.

Step 2. Pin, baste, and sew the other side body piece, right sides of the fabric facing, to the other side of the sewn section of the underbody. Start at A and go around the head and along the back, sewing the tail in firmly at B. Continue down around the legs, leaving an opening of approximately 2½ inches (64 mm) for turning and stuffing between them and up to A again.

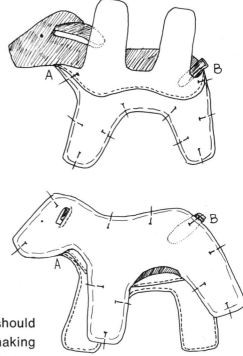

Turning and Stuffing

Turn right side out and stuff. The legs and the head should be a bit more firmly stuffed than the body. If you are making the lamb without the sheep, and intend it to be a cuddle toy, stuff it much less firmly. Close the opening with a small overcast stitch.

Finishing

Embroider the eyes with a satin stitch.

If you have made the mother sheep and this lamb is to go with her, sew a negative snap on the middle of the nose.

Mother Duck and Ducklings

My mother duck has three ducklings, but of course you may give yours as many as you like. With snaps on the ducklings' tail feathers and the tips of their beaks, they will follow her obediently. One little duckling without the snaps makes an engaging and inexpensive little gift on his own.

I used a white fur fabric for the body of the duck and the ducklings with a small-scale printed yellow cotton for the bills, wing linings, and feet. But if you like, you can make the mother duck of printed cotton or terry cloth with plain cotton bill, wing linings, and feet. She isn't quite as plump as she is in fur fabric, but she is still most attractive. The little ducklings always look best if they are fluffy and made in fur fabric.

There is only one place to watch in making the duck. When you cut the holes for the legs, cut a small hole first and increase its size by cutting radiating slits a little at a time so the holes won't get too large.

You will need

- Body fabric for the mother duck, 30 inches by 20 inches (76 cm by 51 cm)
- Body fabric for 3 ducklings, 20 inches by 8 inches (51 cm by 21 cm)
- Cotton for feet, bills, and wing linings for the whole family, 8 inches by 30 inches (21 cm by 76 cm)
- Scraps of felt for tail (optional)
- 2 buttons, ⅝ of an inch (16 mm) in diameter for the mother duck's eyes (optional)
- Embroidery thread or scraps of felt for the ducklings' eyes
- 4 pairs of snaps
- Dacron polyester for stuffing, 8 ounces

The Mother Duck

To draw the patterns, rule lines on wrapping paper across and down 1½ inches apart to make 1½-inch by 1½-inch squares. Copy the patterns onto these squares (see page 10).

Cutting

Lay out the body fabric wrong side up. Place your patterns on it, following the directions of the arrows so the nap (or pattern if you are using a printed cotton) runs from the head to the tail. Cut 2 side bodies, reversing one by flipping it over before you cut the second. Cut 1 underbody. Cut 2 wings of the body fabric and reverse one. Cut 1 tail feather of the body fabric if you are using a fur fabric or terry cloth. If you are using cotton for the body, cut the tail feather from a scrap of matching felt by holding the pattern against the felt between the thumb and forefinger and cutting around it. Do not mark the felt. From the cotton material, cut 2 wings for lining, reversing one, 2 bills, reversing one, and 4 feet.

Mark the As, Bs, etc., the slits in the side bodies for the wings, the slit in the tail feather, and ½-inch (13-mm) circles in the underbody to mark the leg holes. Mark the position of the eyes with a contrasting thread, knotted and pulled through to the right side of the fabric.

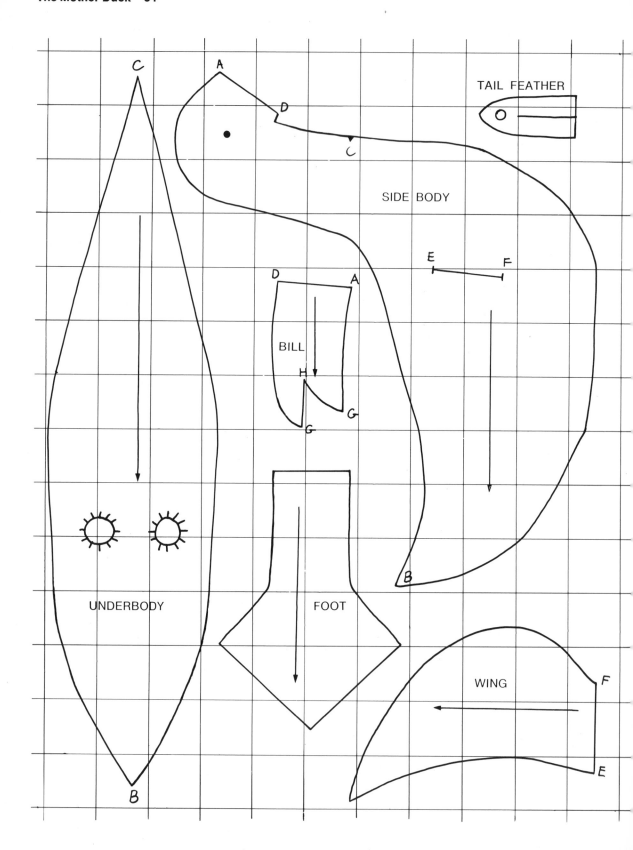

Sewing

All seams should be ³⁄₁₆ of an inch (5 mm).

Step 1. Pin and sew two foot pieces together around the edges, right sides of the fabric facing, leaving the top of the leg open for turning right side out. Before turning, cut close to the seam at the corners of the foot and clip at the ankle. Turn and stuff with Dacron polyester within 1 inch (25 mm) of the top of the leg. Repeat with the other foot.

Step 2. Pin and sew the cotton lining to the wing, right sides of the fabrics facing, leaving the base open for turning. Cut across the tip of the wing close to the seam, clip curves, and then turn. Repeat with the other wing.

Step 3. To sew the bill onto the head, match the A and the D of one bill piece to the A and the D of one of the side body pieces, right sides of the fabrics facing, and pin and sew from A to D. Repeat with the other bill piece and the other side body piece.

Step 4. To attach the wings, cut the wing slits in the side body pieces between E and F. Lay a wing, lining side down, on the right side of the fabric of a side body piece. Match the Es and the Fs so the wing curves upward toward the back. Push the base of the wing through the right side of the fabric so ⅛ of an inch (3 mm) of the base shows on the wrong side and pin in place. Sew firmly on the wrong side of the fabric so the wing is caught between the sides of the slit. Repeat with the other wing and the other side body piece.

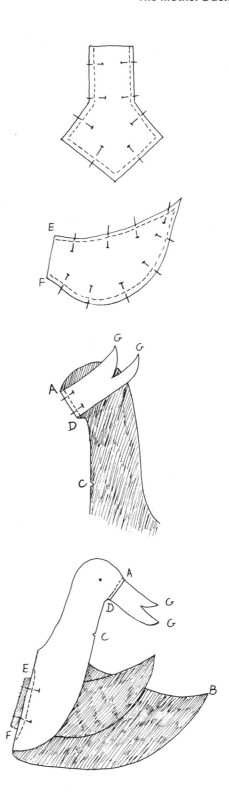

Step 5. To attach the tail feather to the body, first cut the slit in the base of the tail feather, overlap the two ends, and sew across. This gives a natural curl to the tail feather. If you are using a felt tail feather, you can glue the two ends of the slit together. Sew a positive snap on the right side of the fabric near the tip if you are making ducklings to go with the mother duck. Then fold the tail feather lengthwise and baste to the right side of one of the side body pieces just below B. Angle the tail feather down with the right side of the fabric facing up.

Step 6. Cut the two circular leg holes ½ inch (13 mm) in diameter in the underbody. Then sew the underbody to the side body piece to which you have attached the tail, right sides of the fabric facing, first pinning and basting, then sewing from C to B. Just before you get to B, be sure to sew the tail feather into the seam firmly.

Step 7. Next pin, baste, and sew the second side body to the underbody, right sides of the fabric facing, then sew the two side bodies together from G at the tip of the upper bill through A and along the top of the back to B. The seams at A between the duck's bill and the top of her head should match exactly. Then pin, baste, and sew the side to the underbody from B at the tail to C at the throat, leaving a 4-inch (10-cm) opening for turning and stuffing centered over the holes for the feet in the under-body. Continue up the throat, matching the seams at D exactly, and on to G at the tip of the lower bill.

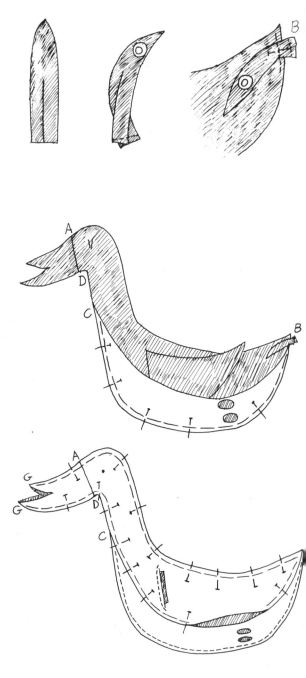

Step 8. Press the top and the bottom of the bill together so the top G matches the bottom G and pin and sew from H to H. Clip the curves of the neck, chest, and of the bill, and cut across the point of the tail at B close to the seam. Now is a good time to check all the seams to make sure they have been sewn securely. Then turn the duck right side out, using the blunt end of a knitting needle to turn the end of the bill and the point at B completely.

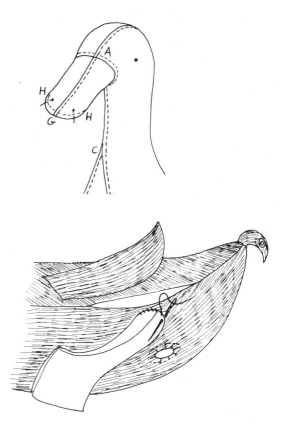

Step 9. Cut small radiating slits out from the leg holes in the underbody. Poke the ends of the legs into the holes ¼ of an inch (6 mm), with the side seams of the legs at right angles to the underbody seam so the feet will face forward. Put your left hand inside the duck through the opening in the side seam and hold the legs in place as you hand-sew the tops of the legs around the holes with small, firm stitches.

Stuffing
When you stuff the duck, be sure to fill up the tops of the legs before you start filling the body. The bill should be flat and the neck should be very firmly stuffed so she holds her head high. Close the opening with small overcast stitches.

Finishing
You can use button eyes (see page 126) or embroider them with a satin stitch or sew on small rounds of felt.

The Ducklings

The ducklings are made just like the mother duck except they are far easier. There are no wings and the bill is simpler. The ducklings have no necks since the underbody goes right up to the bill. The feet are not stuffed and they are sewn into the underbody before the duckling is assembled. The patterns for the duckling are the exact size so they can be traced.

Cutting

For three ducklings: From the fur fabric cut 6 side bodies, reversing three by flipping the pattern over. Cut 3 tail feathers and 3 underbodies. From the cotton cut 6 bills, reversing three, and 12 feet. Mark the As, Bs, and Cs, and the slit for the feet on the underbody. Mark the eyes with contrasting colored thread, knotted and pulled through to the right side of the fabric.

Sewing

Allow ³⁄₁₆ of an inch (5 mm) for the seams.

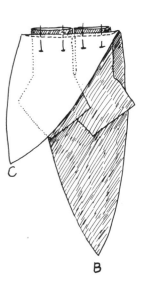

Step 1. Sew and turn the feet as for the mother duck, but do not stuff them. Insert the feet into the slit in the underbody from the right side of the fabric, with the leg seams on the side, and ⅛ of an inch (3 mm) of the tops of the legs showing from the wrong side of the fabric. When you sew across, be sure that both sides of the slit and the tops of the legs are caught together firmly.

For the rest, the procedure is very much like that for the mother duck. Make the tail feather like the mother's and baste it onto the right side of the fabric of one of the side body pieces just below B as in the directions for the mother duck. Sew a positive snap on the tip of the tail feather. Sew on the bill, matching As and Cs, and sew the underbody onto one side body piece from C to B. Then sew on the other side body piece, starting at A, matching the As carefully, and sewing around the bill and through C toward B, leaving an opening of approximately 2½ inches (64 mm) just above the legs for turning and stuffing, and continue to A again.

Cut across the tip of the bill close to the seam and clip the curves. Turn right side out and stuff. Close the opening with a small overcast stitch.

Finishing

Sew a negative snap on the underside of each duckling's bill close to the tip.

For the eyes use ⅛-of-an-inch (3-mm) beads (see page 126) or sew on ⅛-of-an-inch (3-mm) rounds of felt, or embroider eyes with a satin stitch.

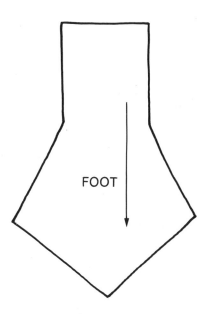

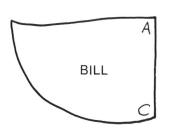

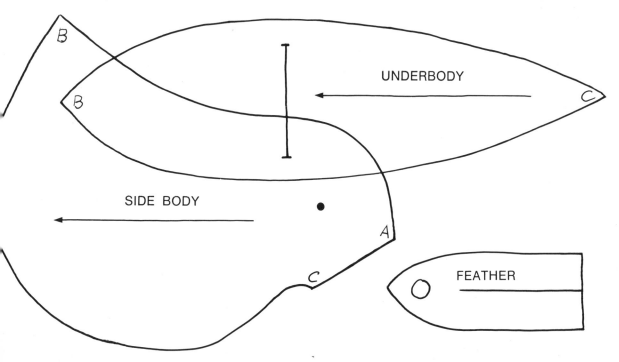

Dolphin

Since I intended this dolphin as a nursery toy, I used a pale blue, frosted, curly-pile fabric for the body, a short-pile, white fur fabric for the underbody, and pink felt for the inside of his mouth. He also makes a fine, wild fantasy toy in bright prints if the scale of the pattern isn't too large.

He is twenty-one inches long, but you can enlarge your grid squares or have the patterns photostated up to a much larger size and he will make an attractive, decorative pillow in velvet or some soft fabric. If you do make him into a pillow, you can use padded felt eyes instead of buttons.

The dolphin is easy to make. His mouth is his main feature —after all, dolphins talk—and it needs a little care, especially at the corners where the jaws meet.

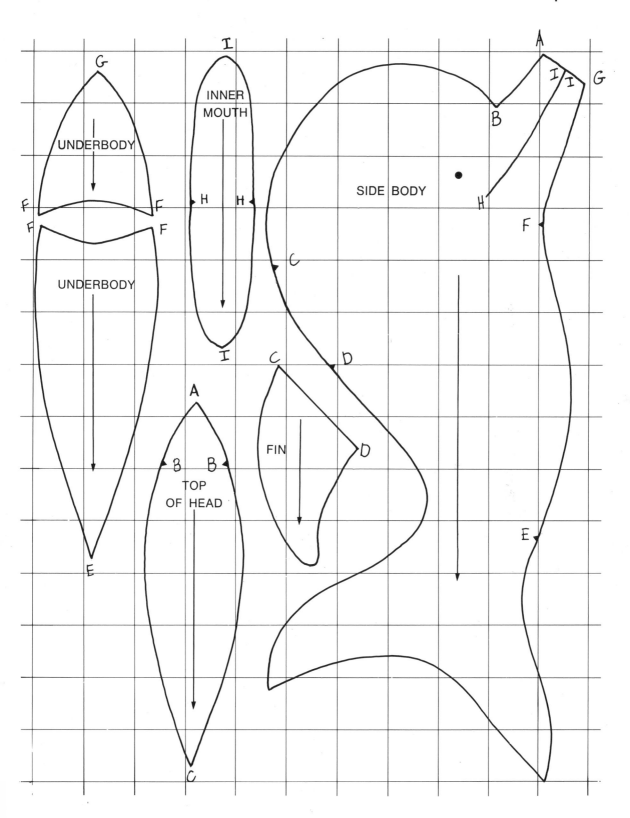

You will need

- Body fabric, 30 inches by 30 inches (76 cm by 76 cm)
- Underbody material, 14 inches by 5 inches (36 cm by 13 cm)
- Felt for the mouth, 9 inches by 3 inches (23 cm by 8 cm)
- 2 flat buttons or scraps of felt for the eyes, ¾ of an inch (19 mm) in diameter
- Dacron polyester for stuffing, approximately 9 ounces

To draw the patterns, rule lines on wrapping paper across and down 1½ inches apart to make 1½-inch by 1½-inch squares. Copy the patterns onto these squares (see page 10).

Cutting

Lay out the body fabric wrong side up. Place your patterns on it, following the directions of the arrows so the nap runs from the head to the tail. From the body fabric cut 2 side bodies, flipping the pattern over to reverse the second. Cut 2 fins, reversing one. Cut 1 top of the head. From the underbody fabric cut 1 each of the two underbody pieces. Cut 1 mouth of felt. Mark the As, Bs, etc. Mark the eyes by pulling a knotted, contrasting colored thread through to the right side of the fabric.

Sewing

All seams should be ¼ of an inch (6 mm).
As the fin pieces are small, sew the fin first and put it aside before assembling the dolphin. Sew the two fin pieces together, right sides of the fabric facing, leaving the space between C and D unsewn for turning. Clip across the point at the tip of the fin close to the seam and turn right side out.

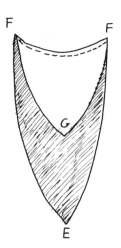

Step 1. Sew the two underbody pieces together, right sides of the fabrics facing, from F to F.

Step 2. First sew the two side body pieces together at the nose, right sides of the fabrics
facing, from A to I on the upper jaw and from
I to G on the lower jaw. Fold the felt mouth
crosswise at the Hs and pin and baste in place,
matching the Hs and Is of the mouth to the Hs
and the Is of the jaws. Sew in place.

Step 3. Pin and baste one side of the top of the
head to one of the side bodies, matching the
As, Bs, and Cs. Sew in place.

Step 4. Baste the fin to the right side of the
fabric on one of the side body pieces between
C and D, matching the Cs and the Ds so the fin
will curve back toward the tail, and leave ⅛ of
an inch (3 mm) of the base of the fin showing on
the wrong side. Then pin and baste the unsewn
side of the top of the head to the other side body
from A through B to C. Continue across the fin
through D and around the tips of the tail to E.
Then sew in one continuous seam. If you are
using a deep-piled fabric and have difficulty in
machine-sewing the fin, you can backstitch
firmly by hand.

Step 5. Pin and baste the underbody from G to
E on both sides, matching the Fs. Leave a
3-inch (8-cm) opening from E toward the mouth
for turning and stuffing. Sew the rest of the
underbody in place.

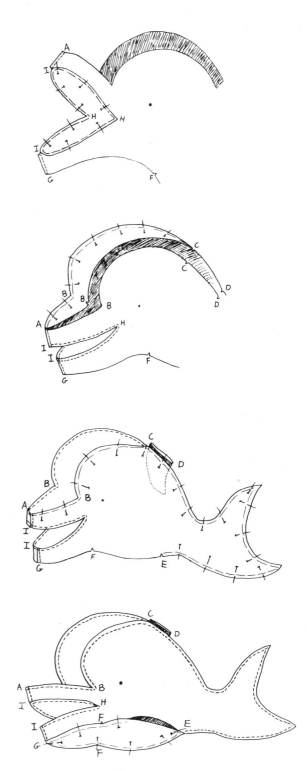

Turning and Stuffing

Clip the curves and angles, taking particular care at the Bs and the Hs. Cut off the tips of the tail close to the seam. Check all seams to see if stitching is secure, and if it isn't, reinforce them by hand. This is especially important at C where the two sides and the top of the head meet. When you turn the dolphin right side out, use the blunt end of a knitting needle or a crochet hook at the tips of the tail so they are thoroughly turned and have nice, precise points.

When you stuff, use small pieces at the tips of the tail and in the jaws. Stuff the tail firmly and keep the under jaw as flat as you can. If the dolphin is made of a fluffy fabric, he is a cuddle toy and the body shouldn't be stuffed too firmly.

Finishing

If the dolphin is made from a fur fabric, brush the seams gently to free any fur which may have been caught in the stitching.

For button eyes, see page 126. For felt eyes, make circles ¾ of an inch (19 mm) in diameter (see page 125). If you decide to use soft fabric eyes, make them 1 inch (25 mm) in diameter (see page 124).

Monkey

This monkey was designed to hug or he can sit neatly on a hip like a baby. He looks handsome in a tipped fur fabric, but since real monkeys come in many colors and textures you can have a lot of fun in choosing a suitable fur fabric. It seems to me that he is more interesting if his body fur fabric and his felt face, palms, and soles of the feet are somewhat contrasted but correlated. If the fur of his body is light, then use a darker felt and vice versa.

This pattern is not for the veriest beginner to tackle, but if you follow the directions carefully and work slowly, you can turn out a magnificent monkey. Watch such details as sewing the thumbs and double-check the rights and lefts when you cut the patterns. As he is fairly large, twenty inches without his tail, and the contours of the seams from the head to the tail are curved, and fur fabric is a bit stretchy, pin carefully before you sew. Pin at the ends of the seams and then pin between, easing and matching the raw edges as you go. He will then be a well-tailored monkey.

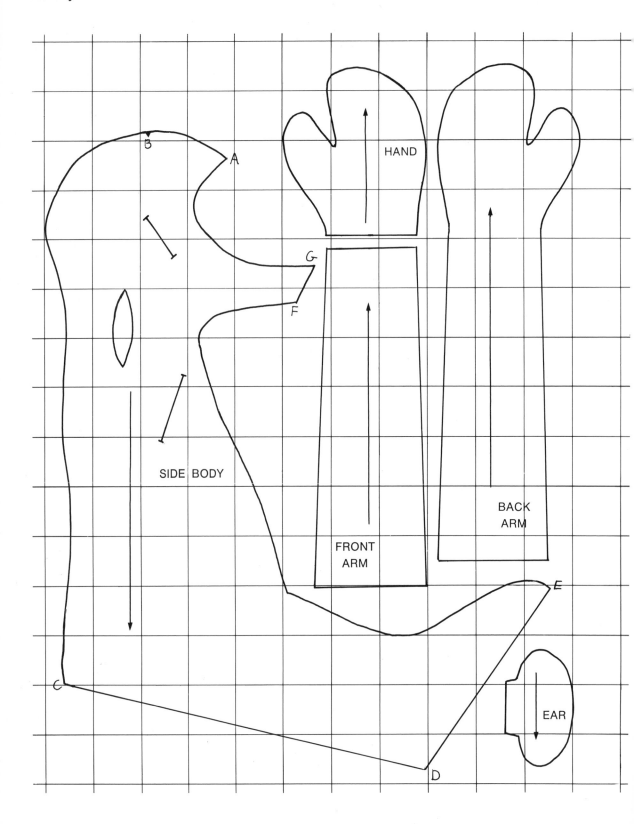

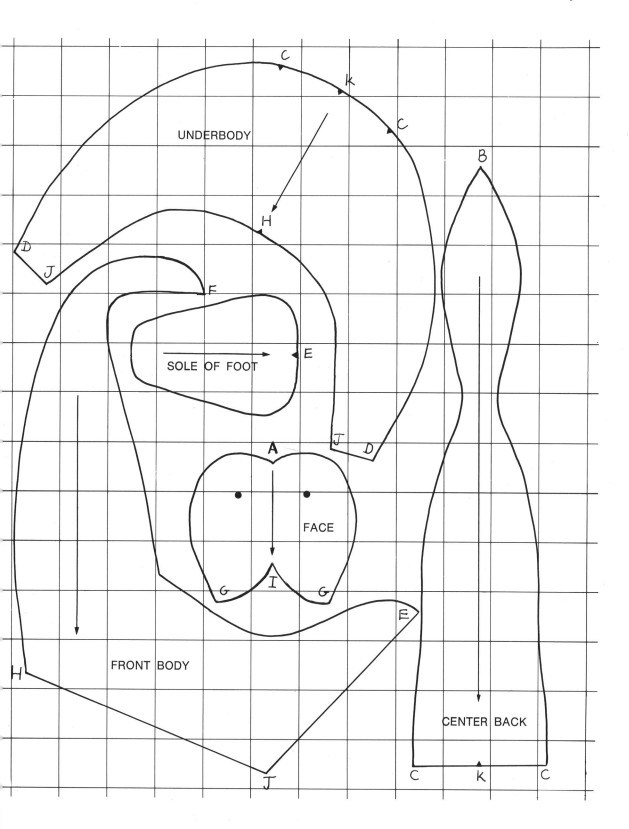

You will need
- Fur fabric for body, ¾ of a yard (69 cm)
- Felt for face, paws, ear linings, and soles of feet, 12 inches by 12 inches (31 cm by 31 cm)
- 2 shiny, black, flattish buttons, ¾ of an inch (19 mm) in diameter, for eyes
- Dacron polyester, nearly 2 pounds, for stuffing

To draw the patterns, rule lines on wrapping paper across and down 1½ inches apart to make 1½-inch by 1½-inch squares. Copy the patterns onto these squares (see page 10).

Cutting

Lay out the fur fabric wrong side up. Place your patterns on it, following the directions of the arrows so the nap runs from the head to the tail. Cut 2 side bodies, flipping the pattern over to reverse the second. Cut 2 front bodies, reversing the second. Cut 2 backs of the arms, reversing the second. Cut 2 ears, reversing the second. Cut 2 front arms, 1 center back, and 1 underbody. Cut 1 tail 4½ inches by 20 inches (11 cm by 51 cm), with the nap running the length.

From the felt cut 1 face, 2 soles of the feet, 2 ears, reversing one, and 2 hands, reversing one.

Mark the As, Bs, etc., the darts, and the ear and arm slits. Mark the position of the eyes on the felt face by pulling a knotted, contrasting colored thread through to the right side of the fabric.

Sewing

All seams should be ¼ of an inch (6 mm). Before you start to put the monkey together, sew the smaller pieces first and put them aside.

Fold the tail in half lengthwise, right sides of the fabric facing, and sew a seam down the length and across the tip. Be sure the nap of the fabric runs toward the tip. Turn the tail right side out. A long dowel or the blunt end of a knitting needle is useful here.

Sew the darts in the neck of the two side body pieces and trim off the excess fabric.

Sew the felt ear linings to the fur fabric ears, right side of the fur fabric facing the felt. Sew around the outline of the ear, leaving the base of the ear unsewn to provide an opening for turning. Clip on curves and turn right side out.

Step 1. Pin and sew the felt palms onto the front arms, the right side of the fur fabric facing the felt. Lay both arms and palms out at the same time so the thumbs are facing each other.

Step 2. Pin, baste, and sew the backs of the arms to the front arms and palms, right sides of the fabric facing. Clip the curves of the hands and turn inside out. Stuff the hands and wrists, but let the stuffing peter out two-thirds of the way up the arm. This will give a freer action to the arms at the shoulders.

Step 3. Cut the ear slits in the side body pieces and poke the base of the ears through them from the right side of the fabric so ⅛ of an inch (3 mm) shows on the wrong side. Be sure that the felt lining faces toward G on the front of the head and that the nap of the fur fabric runs down from the top of the head. Pinch the two sides of the slit together and sew across so the base of the ear is caught firmly on both sides.

Cut the arm slits in the side body pieces, poke the tops of the arms through so ⅛ of an inch (3 mm) shows on the wrong side. Be sure the felt palms face front and that the thumbs stick up. Pinch the two sides of the slits together and sew across so the arms are caught firmly on both sides. If there is too much bulk for your machine, you can backstitch them in firmly by hand.

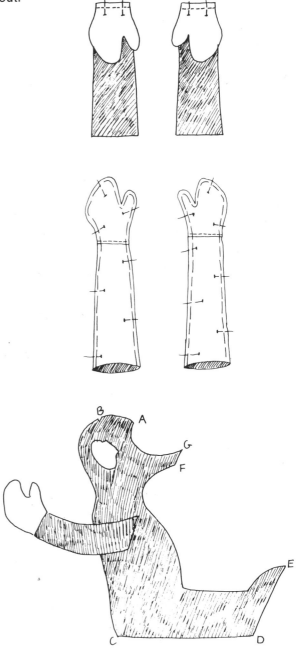

Step 4. Pin and baste the two side body pieces together, right sides of the fabric facing, from A at the center of the forehead to B on the top of the head. Then put in the center back piece by pinning B on the center back to the B on one of the side pieces, right sides of the fabric facing. Continue pinning down both sides of the center back to the two Cs. Ease both seams so they come out even, then baste and sew. Sew one side first from B to C, then sew the other side from A on the forehead to C.

Step 5. Match the A of the face piece to the A of the body at the center of the forehead. Then pin and baste the face piece in place, easing it around the curves to both Gs. Then sew the seam around the face from G to G, leaving the part from the two Gs to I unsewn.

Step 6. Fold the face from A to I, matching the two seams at G exactly. Pin and sew from F through G to I, making a dart by tapering the seam to the fold just above I.

Step 7. Sew the front body pieces together, right sides of the fabric facing, down the center front from F to H. Then pin the outer curves of the front section to the side body pieces, starting at F under the chin to the Es, first one side and then the other. Ease and baste before sewing.

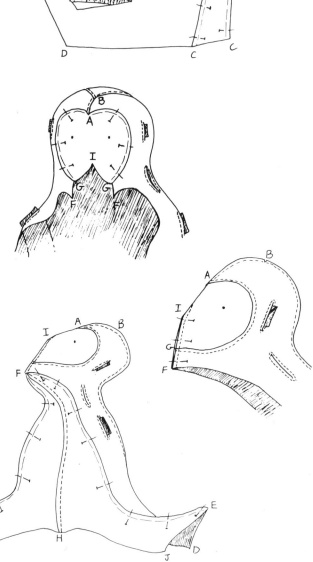

Step 8. Flatten the tail so the seam is in the center and pin it to the right side of the center back piece at K. Be sure the seam faces out so that it will be underneath the tail when the monkey is finished. Sew the tail firmly in place.

Step 9. Before sewing the underbody to the monkey's front and sides, tuck the arms and the tail inside. Match the two Cs and the Hs and pin. Then match the two Ds and two Js and pin. Pin, baste, and sew from C through the other C to D at the outer heel. Then pin, baste, and sew from J at the inner heel through H at the center of the stomach and to the other J. Pin and baste from D toward C on the other side, leaving an opening of around 5 inches (13 cm) for turning and stuffing.

Step 10. Place the felt sole of the foot with the center of the heel between D and J, matching the Es at the center of the toes. Pin, baste, and sew around the sole. Repeat with the other foot.

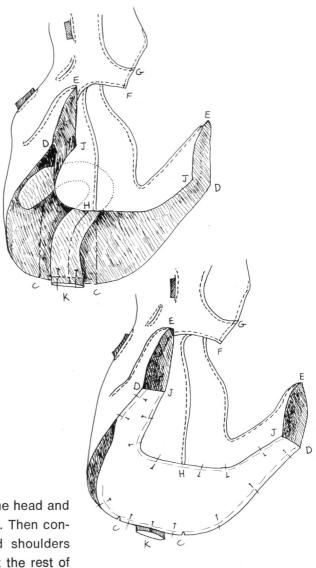

Turning and Stuffing

Clip all the curves and turn right side out. Stuff the head and the neck thoroughly, shaping the face as you go. Then continue with handful-sized pieces. The neck and shoulders should be solidly stuffed so the neck is firm, but the rest of the body should have some give so your monkey will be pleasingly huggable. You can judge this by feel as you go. Make the stuffing at the bottom flat so he will sit up. Close the opening with small overcast stitches.

Finishing

Gently brush out any fur that is caught in the seams and then brush all over with the nap of the fabric.

See page 126 for sewing on the button eyes. I stem-stitched a mouth on my monkey but did not give him any nostrils. Perhaps you would like to add nostrils.

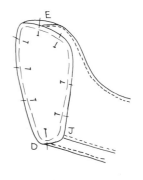

Rainbow Dolls and Dancing Mice

I call these rainbow dolls because I first did them in rainbow colors—blue, green, yellow, pink, and lavender. But there are endless combinations of colors and correlated prints you may use. The skirt of one can match the hat of another, for example. So just mix and match as you wish.

It isn't necessary to make five snap-together dolls as I did. A single doll in an arabesque can snap her hands together. Two can dance hand in hand or you can make a circle of three. That's why I've given the fabric requirements for only one doll.

I kept them very simple and abstract without eyes or mouths as I rather prefer them that way and I was thinking of Matisse's dancers when I designed them. But of course you may add embroidered mouths and embroidered or button eyes. Or you might want to use the same body pattern to make the dancing mice on page 79.

The rainbow dolls are not particularly hard to make as they are only twelve inches high. They just take care and accurate sewing. I think in some ways the turning and the stuffing are the fussiest part. Since they are done in smooth cotton, you have to turn them carefully, use very small pieces of stuffing, and work slowly so there won't be any lumps.

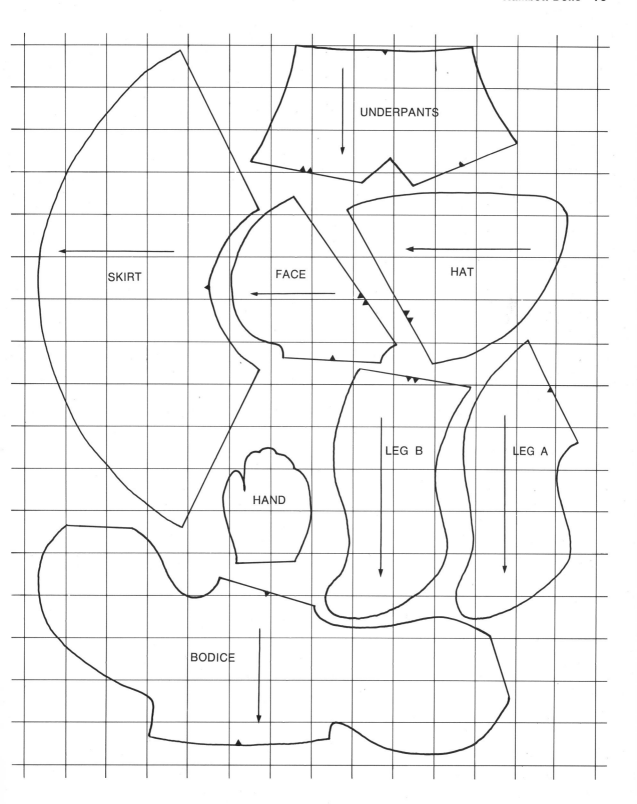

UNDERPANTS

SKIRT

FACE

HAT

LEG B

LEG A

HAND

BODICE

Rainbow Dolls

You will need for one doll

- Solid pastel cotton for hands, legs, and face, 14 inches by 14 inches (36 cm by 36 cm)
- A printed, coordinated cotton for dress, underpants, and hat, 24 inches by 16 inches (61 cm by 41 cm)
- Medium snaps, 1 pair
- Dacron polyester for stuffing, approximately 6 ounces

To draw the pattern, rule lines on wrapping paper across and down 1 inch apart to make 1-inch by 1-inch squares. Copy the pattern onto these squares (see page 10).

Cutting

Fold the plain material double, right sides of the fabric facing, and cut the patterns two at a time. Place your patterns on the fabric, following the directions of the arrows so the grain runs from the head to the feet. Cut 2 pairs of hands, reversing one pair. Cut 2 legs A and 2 legs B. Cut 2 faces.

Fold the printed material double, right sides of the fabric facing. Lay your patterns on the fabric following the directions of the arrows for the design or grain of the fabric. Cut 2 bodices, 2 skirts, 2 hats, and 2 pairs of underpants.

Mark the single and double marks with tiny single and double snips or with a felt-tip pen.

The only tricky part in putting this doll together is making sure not to get a hand or leg on backward, which is easy to do if you are working in a hurry. A foolproof way to avoid this is to lay out all the pieces for both sides of the doll, wrong side of the fabric up, as in the drawing. Then pin the top pieces together, hands to wrists, face to neck of bodice, and cap on head. Then pin legs and underpants together, but leave the waist unpinned since the top and the bottom sections are put together last. For clarity's sake, I've drawn large notches on the illustrations rather than the small snips or marks you will be using.

Check to see that the two sides are mirror images of each other, that the thumbs of the hands are nearest the head, the upraised arm is toward the face, the upraised leg is toward the back, and that the caps point the right way.

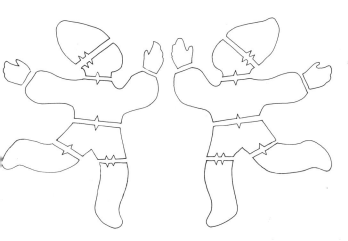

Sewing

All seams should be ³⁄₁₆ of an inch (5 mm).

Step 1. Pin and sew the four hand pieces to the wrists of the bodices, right sides of the fabrics facing. Then pin and sew the two face pieces to the bodices at the neck lines, matching the single marks, right sides of the fabrics facing.

Step 2. Pin and sew the two hat pieces to the tops of the foreheads, matching the double marks.

Step 3. Pin and sew the two top halves of the body together, the right sides of the fabrics facing, leaving the waist unsewn for turning. Try to match the seams at the foreheads, necks, and wrists as carefully as possible.

Clip the curves and the angles and cut across the tips of the thumbs and the peak of the hat close to the seams. Check the seams for any missing stitches. Turn right side out. Use a crochet hook or an orange stick at the peak of the hat and the tips of the thumbs so they are completely turned.

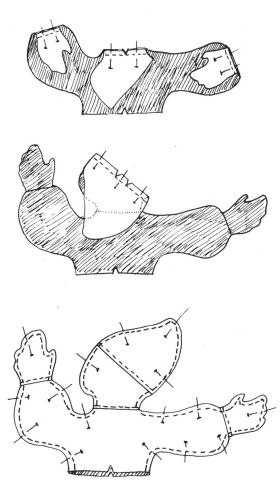

Step 4. Pin and sew the four leg pieces onto the underpant pieces, right sides of the fabrics facing, matching the single and double marks.

Step 5. Pin and sew the two bottom halves of the body together, right sides of the fabrics facing, leaving the waist unsewn for turning. Match the seams where the legs and the underpants join as carefully as possible. Clip the curves and the angles and cut across the tips of the toes close to the seams. Check for missing stitches and turn right side out. Use a crochet hook or an orange stick at the tips of the toes and on the heels so they are completely turned.

Step 6. Pin and sew the side seams of the skirt. Press seams and hem with a hand roll.

Step 7. Slip the skirt over the top half of the doll like a lampshade with the wrong side facing out. Pin the side seams of the skirt to the side seams of the doll at the waistline. Then pin, baste, and sew the skirt to the top half of the doll around the waistline.

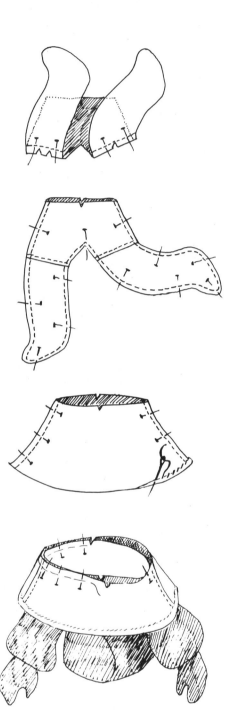

Step 8. To join the top and bottom halves, pin them together at the waist with the wrong side of the skirt to the right side of the underpants. Match the side seams, then pin and baste from side seam to side seam, leaving the other side open for turning and stuffing. Sew the seam *below* the seam where the skirt is sewn to the bodice, and before you sew, check to see that the toes and the face are pointing in the same direction.

Stuffing

Since these dolls are made of smooth cotton and every lump will show, they should be stuffed carefully with very small pieces. The thumbs and the toes need special care, and the neck should be stuffed very firmly so the head won't sag. After stuffing, close the opening under the skirt with small overcast stitches.

Finishing

Sew snaps to the hands on the inside of the palm on one hand and the back of the hand on the other so one can clap hands, two can dance together, and more can form a circle.

Dancing Mice

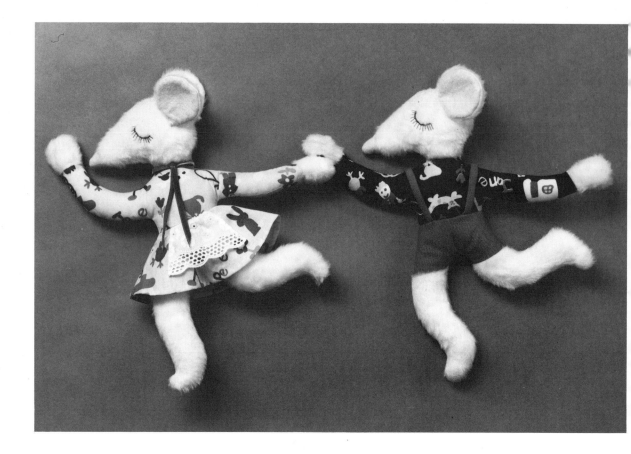

The dancing mice are a whimsical variation on the rainbow dolls. They are made with the same body patterns and by the same method. Only the hands and head are cut differently. A fur fabric, if it is lightweight with a short nap, is ideal for the heads, legs, and hands, or you can use wool or a brushed flannel or velveteen. The only tricky spot in making them is in turning the heads since the necks are narrow.

I chose to embroider the eyes shut with long lashes, but button eyes are equally nice. There is a lot of scope in dressing these dolls—aprons, bows, lace at throat and sleeves, tiny buttons on the dress. You can really let yourself go.

You will need for the pair of dancing mice

- Fabric for heads, hands, legs, and ears, 18 inches by 17 inches (46 cm by 43 cm)
- Pink felt for nose and ear linings, 8 inches by 8 inches (21 cm by 21 cm)
- Printed cotton for bodices and girl mouse's skirt and under-pants, 25 inches by 20 inches (64 cm by 51 cm)
- Solid-colored cotton for boy mouse's underpants, 8 inches by 8 inches (21 cm by 21 cm)
- Embroidery thread, dark gray or brown, for eyes (optional)
- 2 buttons, flat and ⅝ of an inch (16 mm) in diameter, for eyes
- Scrap of embroidery for apron (optional)
- Thin velvet or grosgrain ribbon for girl mouse (optional)
- Medium snaps, 2 pairs
- Dacron polyester for stuffing, approximately 12 ounces for both

Follow the rainbow doll pattern for legs, underpants, bodice, and skirt, but use the dancing mice patterns for the heads, noses, hands, ears, and ear linings. The grid for these patterns should be drawn in 1-inch squares.

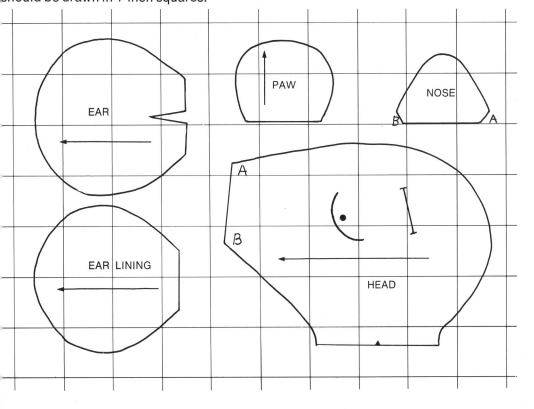

If you are embroidering eyelashes, mark the curve on the head with a running stitch in a contrasting colored thread, pulling it through to the right side of the fabric. If you are using button eyes, mark the eye dot by pulling through a knotted, contrasting colored thread.

Sewing

All seams should be ³/₁₆ of an inch (5 mm).

First, working on the wrong side of the fabric, sew the darts in the ears. Then line the ears, leaving the base of the ear open for turning. Clip the curves and turn right side out.

Sew the felt nose pieces to the head pieces from A to B, right sides of the fabrics facing.

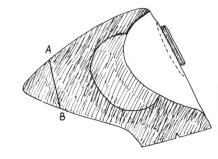

Step 1. Cut the ear slits in the head pieces. Push the base of the ears through the ear slits from the right side of the fabric with the lining against the face so ⅛ of an inch (3 mm) of the base shows from the wrong side. Make sure the lining of the ear faces toward the nose. Pinch the slit together and sew across firmly so both sides are caught in the seam.

From here on follow the procedures for the rainbow dolls. If you wish to give the girl mouse an apron, baste it to the skirt before sewing the skirt on.

Finishing

The eyes can be flat buttons or demurely shut with eyelashes embroidered on.

For button eyes, see page 126.

For embroidered eyelashes, stitch a half circle in stem stitch for the line of the eyelid, using three strands of embroidery thread. Then embroider the eyelashes with a series of radiating stitches in a single strand of thread starting just back of the stem-stitch line. It is easier to make them even by doing the outer ones and the middle one first.

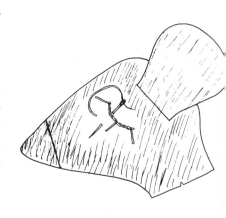

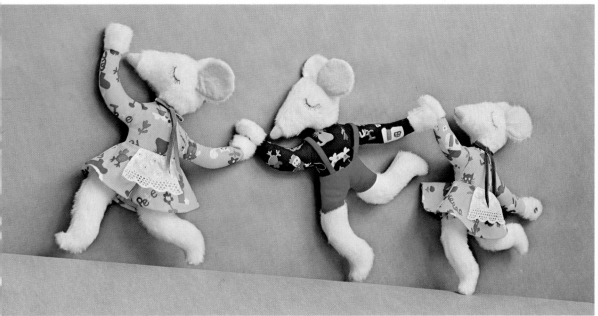

Rainbow dolls in a range of five shades. Sometimes I make a trio of dancing mice instead of a pair.

This group of toys will give you an idea of their various sizes.

A hungry bunny with a calico carrot

Hungry Bunny

The bunny in the photograph was made in a spring green, curly-pile fabric with a white fur fabric underbody and ear linings, but he is just as effective in a coarse tweed, a bouclé wool, or any fleecy fabric. And of course in any colors you choose. He is fine in terry cloth too, though it is not as rich looking. I like to do the snap-on carrot in a small print with an orange or light red background, but you can make a more realistic one of orange felt.

The ears were designed so they can be wired or not, whichever you wish. Wired ears stand up in a jaunty fashion and can be bent into different positions which will vary the bunny's expression. The wiring isn't difficult; it just takes a little more time. Of course if your bunny is intended for a baby, the ears shouldn't be wired.

I decided not to give mine whiskers or a mouth, but if you would like to add whiskers, I would suggest making them of a soft, fine wool or crochet silk which go nicely with his scale as he stands thirteen inches high. And you can stem-stitch a mouth.

You will need

- Body fabric, 20 inches by 30 inches (51 cm by 76 cm)
- Ear lining and underbody fabric, 15 inches by 15 inches (38 cm by 38cm)
- Orange felt or cotton print for carrot, 12 inches by 12 inches (31 cm by 31 cm)
- Green felt for carrot leaves
- 2 buttons for the eyes, ¾ of an inch (19 cm) in diameter (optional)
- Felt for eyes (optional)
- 2 pairs of medium snaps for paws and carrot
- Embroidery wool or crochet silk for nose and whiskers (optional)
- Bias tape for wrapping wire (optional)
- Dacron polyester for stuffing, 11 ounces

To draw the patterns, rule lines on wrapping paper across and down 1½ inches apart to make 1½-inch by 1½-inch squares. Copy the patterns on these squares (see page 10).

When you draw these patterns, the side body pattern and the front body pattern should match. There is a very easy way to do this. Draw around the entire outline of the side body pattern, including the polka-dotted area of the legs and stomach. Then draw the curved line at the side of the polka-dotted area on your pattern.

Before you cut this pattern, place it over another sheet of paper and cut two identical ones around the outside lines. At this time, pay no attention to the curved line that marks the polka-dotted area.

The paper pattern of the whole side of the bunny without the curved line marking off the polka-dotted area is your side body pattern. Then take the paper pattern with the curved line drawn on it and cut along the curve. Discard the back portion, and the front with the legs and stomach is your front body pattern. You now have perfect matches which make sewing the seams much easier and will produce neatly formed legs.

Mark the As, Bs, etc., and pull a knotted, contrasting colored thread through to the right side of the fabric to mark the eyes.

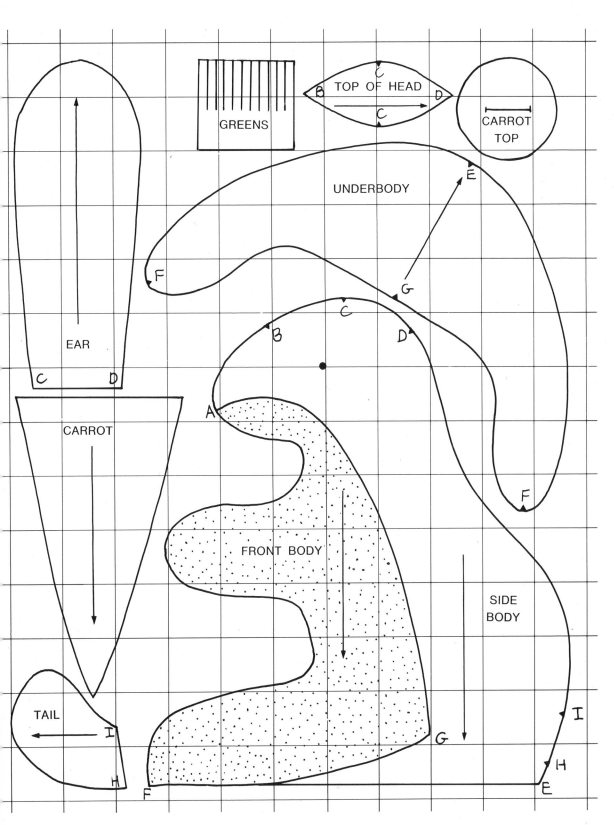

GREENS

TOP OF HEAD

B
C
C
D

CARROT
TOP

UNDERBODY

E

F

G

EAR

C   D

C

B

D

A

CARROT

F

FRONT BODY

SIDE
BODY

TAIL

I

G

I

H

H
F   E

Cutting

Lay out the body fabric wrong side up. Place your patterns on it, following the directions of the arrows so the nap runs from the nose to the tail. Cut 2 side bodies, flipping the pattern over to reverse the second. Cut 2 front bodies, reversing the second, and 2 tails, reversing the second. Cut 1 underbody. Cut 2 ears and 2 ear linings, and 2 carrots, 1 carrot top, and leaves from the felt.

Sewing

All seams should be ¾₆ of an inch (5 mm).

If you are not wiring the ears, sew the linings in, right sides of the fabrics facing, around the ear from C to D, leaving the base of the ear unsewn for turning. Clip the curves and turn right side out. Sew the two tail pieces together, right sides of the fabric facing, leaving the base open for turning. Clip on the curve at the tail tip and turn right side out.

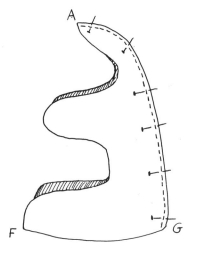

Step 1. Pin and sew the two front body pieces together, right sides of the fabric facing, from A to G as in the drawing.

Step 2. Pin, baste, and sew one side body piece to the front body, right sides of the fabric facing, from A at the tip of the nose to F at the bottom of the hind paws, matching the paws carefully.

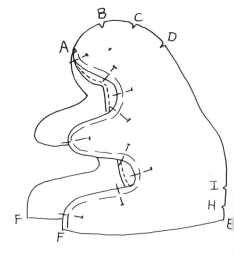

Step 3. Pin, baste, and sew the other side piece to the front body piece, right sides of the fabric facing, from A to F, again matching the paws carefully.

Step 4. If you are not using wired ears, pin and baste the ears onto the right side of the fabric of the side body pieces between C and D, with the lining against the side body piece. ⅛ of an inch (3 mm) of the base of the ears should show from the wrong side so they will be sewn into the seams securely.

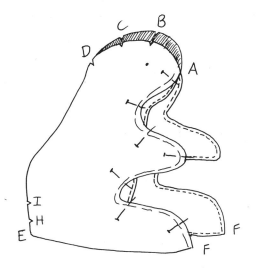

Step 5. Pin and baste the top of the head piece to one side body piece, right sides of the fabric facing, matching the Bs, Cs, and Ds. If you are using wired ears, leave the space between C and D open so the wired ears can be sewn in by hand after the bunny is turned right side out.

If you are sewing unwired ears in and are using a thick-piled fabric and have trouble machine-stitching, sew them by hand with a firm backstitch.

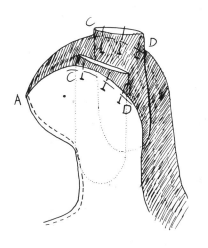

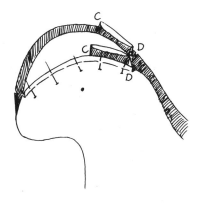

Step 6. Baste the tail in place on the right side of the fabric of one of the side body pieces between H and I so only ⅛ of an inch (3 mm) shows from the wrong side. Place it so the tip curves up toward the head of the bunny.

Then pin and baste the two side bodies together from A at the tip of the nose to B. Continue along the unsewn side of the top of the head to D and go down the center of the back to E. When you sew the seam, start at A, and if you have trouble machine-stitching over the ear or the tail, you can backstitch them in firmly by hand. Again, if you are using wired ears, leave the space between C and D open.

Step 7. Pin and baste the underbody to the body, right sides of the fabric facing, matching the two Fs and the Es. Sew from E through the two Fs at the front of the hind paws and back toward E, leaving an opening of approximately 4 inches (10 cm) before E for turning and stuffing.

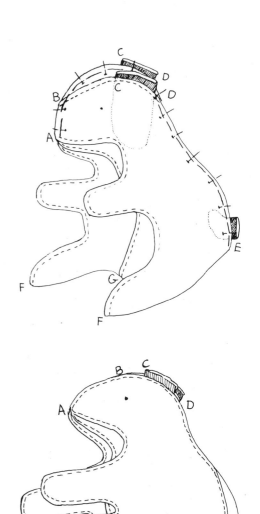

Turning and Stuffing

Clip the curves on the paws and the head. Check the seams to see if there are any missing stitches which should be reinforced by hand sewing. Then turn the bunny right side out.

If you are wiring the ears, they should be wired, lined, and sewn in by hand after the bunny is turned and before it is stuffed.

As the bunny is a cuddly toy, he should not be stuffed too firmly. After stuffing, close the opening with a small overcast stitch.

Finishing

If you are using buttons for the eyes, see page 126. And if you are making soft fabric eyes, see page 124.

If you wish you can satin-stitch the nose and form the outlines of the mouth with a stem stitch or a small chain stitch on the seams where the front body and the side body pieces are sewn together.

The whiskers can be done with embroidery wool or crochet silk. For making them, see page 127.

Wiring the Ears

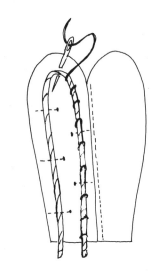

Step 1. Sew the lining up one side of the ear almost to the curve at the top but do not finish the lining. Cut the wire in two and bend the ends of each piece back in small loops. Bend the two pieces in deep Us and wrap them with bias tape. Place the Us of the wire between the ear lining and the ear with 1 inch (25 mm) protruding below the base of the ear. Slip-stitch it to the wrong side of the fabric of the ear underneath the lining. Finish sewing the lining to the ear with small overcast stitches.

Step 2. Insert the ears between C and D at the top of the head, with the lining facing out from the top of the head. Catch the loops of wire firmly to the inside of the head with small stitches, then overcast the base of the ear to the head on both sides to close the opening.

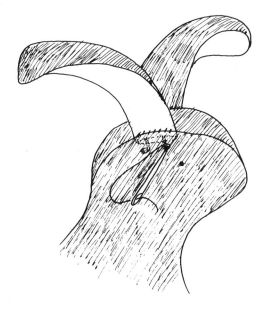

The Carrot

Step 1. Sew the two sides of the carrot together, right sides of the fabric facing, leaving the wide end unsewn for turning. Cut across the tip close to the seam and then turn.

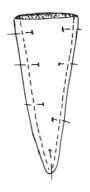

Step 2. Cut the green felt in a fringe to give a leafy effect, make a slit in the carrot top and push the base of the leaves through from the right side of the fabric. Sew it on firmly on the wrong side of the fabric on both sides of the slit.

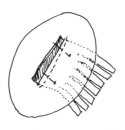

Step 3. Stuff the carrot and hand-sew the top to the bottom with small stitches. Sew negative snaps on each side of the carrot and sew the positive snaps on the tips of the front paws of the bunny.

Honey Bear

This honey bear is a fairly simple and very cuddly teddy bear and he is best made in a furry fabric. Besides the range of the natural colors from white through fawn, beige, apricot, browns, and black, he is also charming in fantasy colors— pale blue, pink, or lavender. A most adaptable bear! I made him in a soft, cream-colored fabric with a fairly long pile and tied a satin ribbon around his neck.

If you follow the dimensions on the grid, he will be fourteen inches high, but he also looks very nice in larger sizes. You might want to double the size of the grid squares you draw and make him twenty-eight inches high. Or you can take this book to a photostater and have the patterns increased to whatever size you wish.

I gave my bear a felt nose but did not add a mouth. You might prefer him with a satin-stitch nose and a mouth done in stem stitch.

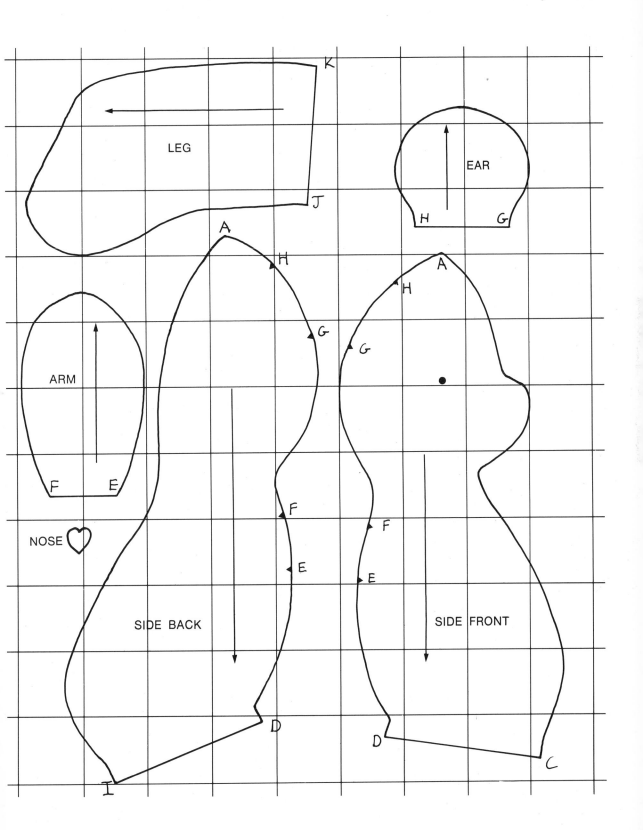

You will need

- Body fabric, 45 inches by 15 inches (114 cm by 38 cm)
- Felt for the nose, a scrap (optional)
- Embroidery thread for the nose (optional)
- 2 flat buttons for the eyes, ¾ of an inch (19 mm) in diameter
- Ribbon for the neck, 30 inches (76 cm) (optional)
- Dacron polyester for stuffing, 8 ounces

To draw the patterns, rule lines on wrapping paper across and down 1½ inches apart to make 1½-inch by 1½-inch squares (see page 10).

Cutting

Lay out the body fabric wrong side up. Place your patterns on it, following the directions of the arrows so the nap runs from the head to the tail. Cut 2 side front bodies, flipping the pattern over to reverse the second. Cut 2 side back bodies, reversing one. Cut 4 legs, reversing two. Cut 4 arms and 4 ears. If you wish a felt nose, cut 1 but do not draw on the felt as it will be sewn on last. Instead, hold the pattern against the felt and cut around it.

Mark the As, Bs, etc., and mark the position of the eyes by pulling a knotted, contrasting colored thread through to the right side of the fabric.

Sewing

All seams should be ¼ of an inch (6 mm). It is a good idea to sew the smaller pieces and put them aside before you assemble the bear. They don't get lost and everything goes much faster at the end.

Pin and sew the ears, placing two pieces together, right sides of the fabric facing, leaving the base open from H to G for turning. Clip the curves and turn right side out.

Pin and sew the arms by placing two pieces together, right sides of the fabric facing, and sew around from E to F, leaving the top of the arms between E and F unsewn for turning. Clip the curves, turn, and stuff the arms lightly, particularly at the tops where they join the body, so they will be flexible.

Step 1. Sew the center back seam by putting the two side back pieces together, right sides of the fabrics facing. Pin, baste, and sew from A to I.

Step 2. Sew the center front seam by putting the two side front pieces together, right sides of the fabric facing. Pin, baste, and sew from A to C. When you go around his nose, take special pains to make the seam allowance exact as the shape of the nose is what gives the bear his appealing expression.

Step 3. Spread out the back of the bear with the right side of the fabric up. Place the ears between H and G, with the base of the ears extended ⅛ of an inch (3 mm) beyond the head, and baste between G and H. Place the arms between E and F in the same way. Point them in matching downward angles and baste them on between E and F.

Step 4. Place the front of the bear against the back, right sides of the fabric facing, and pin, baste, and sew from D up the side through the base of the arms and the ears, over the head, matching the seams at A, and down the other side to D. If you have difficulty machine-sewing in the arms and the ears, you can hand-back-stitch very firmly.

  Clip the curves, with particular attention to the nose. Check the seams to see that they are all sewn securely and turn the bear right side out.

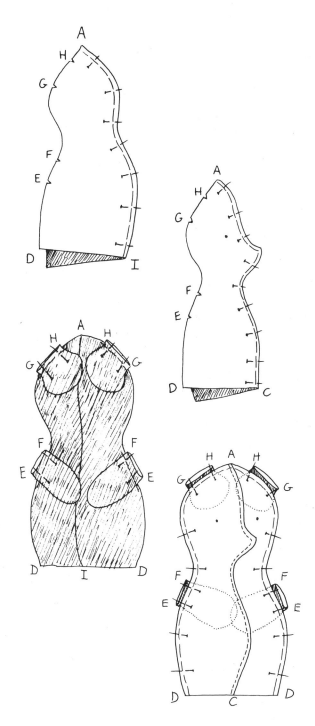

Step 5. Pin and sew two leg pieces together, right sides of the fabric facing. Sew around the leg from J to K, leaving an opening of around 2½ inches (64 mm) above the heel for stuffing. Leave the top between J and K open. Clip the curves at the toe and turn right side out. Repeat with the other two leg pieces.

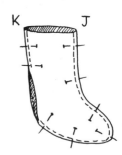

Step 6. To make the toes point forward, fold the legs at the tops so that the seams at the Js and the Ks come together and are centered on the leg. Baste across at the top to secure the seams in this position. Then pin, baste, and sew the tops of the legs to the front section of the bear from D through C to D on the right side of the fabric. *Before you sew,* be sure that the toes are pointing toward the body.

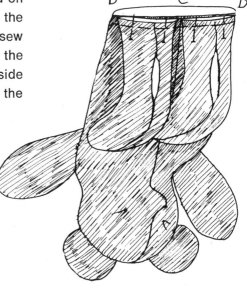

Step 7. Stuff the legs, using less filling toward the tops where they join the body so they can move freely. Close the openings with a small overcast stitch.

Stuff the body medium firm as the honey bear should be squeezable, but stuff the head and neck firmly. When the bear is almost completely filled, start to close the opening. Turning the legs down automatically folds in the raw edge across the front, but on the back you must turn the raw edge in as you close the opening. Continue stuffing with small pieces as you overcast across the opening.

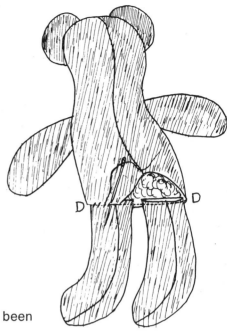

Finishing

Brush the seams gently to free any fur that may have been trapped.

If you are using a felt nose, sew it on with a fine overcast stitch. Or embroider the nose with a satin stitch. If you prefer to give your bear a more realistic look, embroider a mouth with a stem stitch.

Sew on the button eyes (see page 126).

Then tie his bow.

Elephants

I've always loved the playful dignity of elephants. They are so good-humored and patient and I tried to catch these qualities in this design.

For these three—the tips of the trunks and the ends of the tails can be snapped together—I used a creamy suede. But they can be made in numerous fabrics, felt, corduroy, flannel, tweed, or ultrasuede. In fact, anything you wish so long as it is not deeply piled or fleecy. And of course you can make a single elephant without snaps or a pair with snaps on the tips of their trunks and the ends of their tails. These elephants are nine inches high, but they enlarge well and can be very impressive in bigger sizes.

Since these elephants' right sides and left sides are different, which gives them a feeling of motion, the patterns look far more difficult than they are. If you follow the layout, you will find that making them is surprisingly easy.

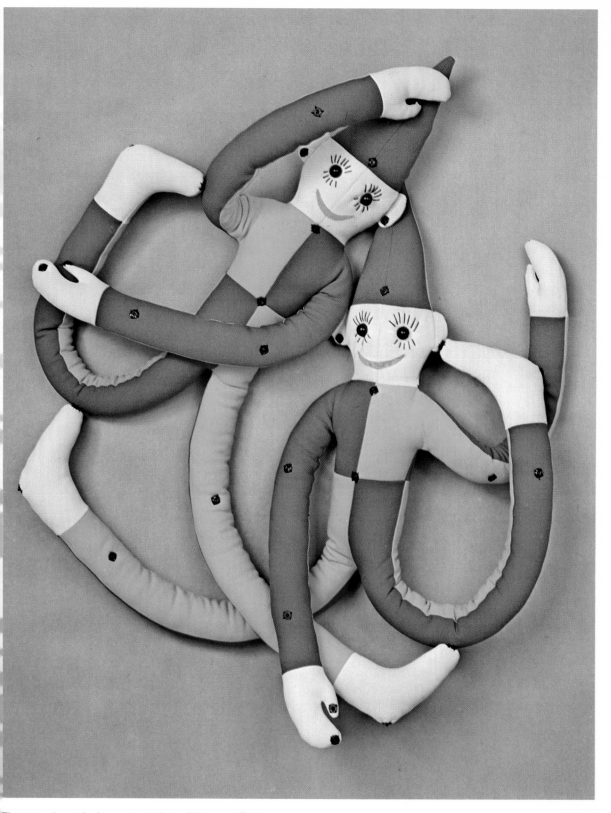

The pretzel people demonstrate their skills as acrobats.

I enjoyed designing these elephants so much I decided to go all out and do them in suede.

Betsey Beagle and her puppies

You will need for one elephant
- Body fabric, 26 inches by 24 inches (66 cm by 61 cm)
- Lining material for ears and tail (optional)
- 2 beads for eyes, ¼ of an inch (6 mm) in diameter (optional)
- Embroidery thread for eyes (optional)
- 1 pair of snaps, medium size (optional)
- Dacron polyester for stuffing, 8 ounces

To draw the patterns, rule lines on wrapping paper across and down 1½ inches apart to make 1½-inch by 1½-inch squares. Copy the patterns onto these squares (see page 10).

Drawing the patterns for the elephant's two different sides is nowhere as difficult as it looks. The side body pattern #1 and the underbody pattern #1 should match. And the side body pattern #2 and the underbody pattern #2 should also match. There is an easy way to do this. Draw around the entire outline of the side body pattern #1, including the polka-dotted area of the legs and stomach. Then draw the curved line at the top of the polka-dotted area across your pattern.

Before you cut this pattern, place it over another sheet of paper and cut around the outside lines, making two identical patterns. The pattern of the whole elephant without the curved line over the polka-dotted area is your side body pattern #1. Now take the paper pattern with the curved line drawn on it and cut along the curve. Discard the upper portion and the lower half is your underbody pattern #1.

Then draw the whole outline for the side body #2. Reverse the underbody #1 pattern and use it for drawing the curved line on underbody #2. Again cut this pattern from double thicknesses of paper. And again the whole outline of the elephant will be your side body #2 pattern. Cut along the curved line and the lower half will be your underbody #2 pattern.

This will ensure perfect matches on all the seams when you put the elephant together.

If you are lining the tail and the ears, draw the outlines of these patterns ³⁄₁₆ of an inch (5 mm) larger all around except for the base for seam allowance. And if the soles of the feet are to be inset and sewn before the elephant is turned, draw the outlines of this pattern ³⁄₁₆ of an inch (5 mm) larger all around.

Cutting

Since the two sides of the elephant are different, it is safer, if you are using a napped fabric, to follow the sketch when you are laying out your pattern for the body pieces.

Lay out the body fabric wrong side up. Place your patterns on it, following the directions of the arrows so the nap runs from the nose to the tail. Cut 1 side body #1 and 1 side body #2. Cut 1 underbody #1 and 1 underbody #2. Cut 2 ears, reversing one, cut 4 soles of the feet, 1 tail, and 1 tip of the trunk.

If you are lining the ears and the tail, cut 2 ears from the lining fabric, reversing one, and 1 tail.

Mark the As, Bs, etc., mark the ear slits, and mark the position of the eye by pulling a knotted, contrasting colored thread through to the right side of the fabric.

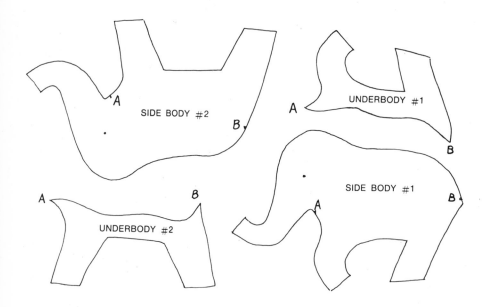

Sewing

All seams should be ³⁄₁₆ of an inch (5 mm).

If you are lining the ears and the tail, sew the linings on, right sides of the fabrics facing, by seaming around the edges, leaving the bases open for turning. Clip the curves of the ears and the tip of the tail and turn them right side out.

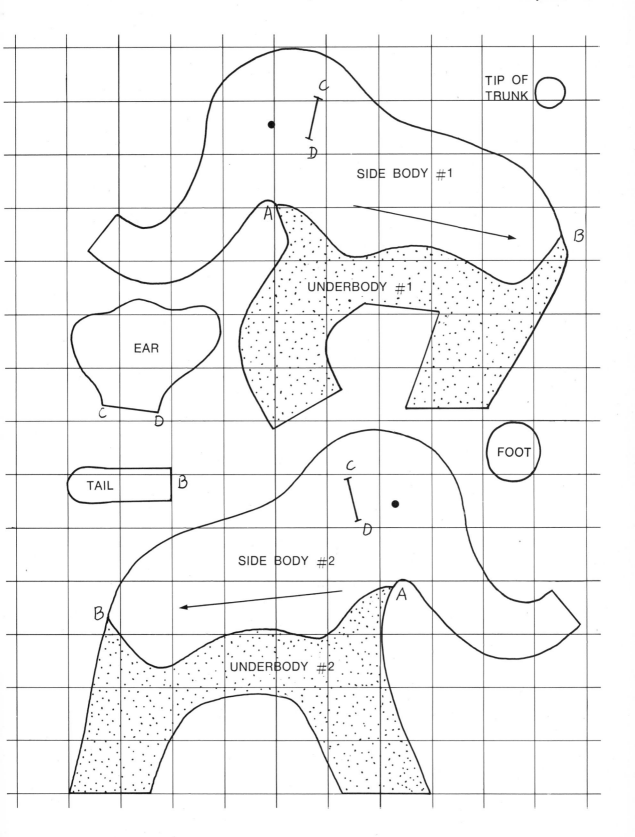

Step 1. Cut the slits for the ears between C and D in the side body pieces. Pleat the ear at C as shown in the drawing. Poke the ear through the ear slit from the right side of the fabric with C toward the top of the head so ⅛ of an inch (3 mm) of the base of the ear shows on the wrong side. If you have lined the ear, the lining should face toward the elephant's trunk. If you are using suede or ultrasuede, the wrong side of the fabric should face the elephant's trunk. Sew the ear in firmly on the wrong side, catching both sides of the slit. Repeat with the other ear.

Step 2. Fold the tail in half lengthwise with the lining, if you have lined it, on the inside, and tack to a side body piece on the right side of the fabric just above B so ⅛ of an inch (3 mm) of the base will show from the wrong side of the fabric. If you are using suede or ultrasuede, the wrong side should be inside the fold.

Step 3. Pin and sew the two underbody pieces together from A where the trunk starts to B at the tail, with the right sides of the fabric facing.

Step 4. Pin, baste, and sew underbody #1 to side body #1, the right sides of the fabric facing, from B to the heel of the hind leg. Then pin and sew from the toe of the hind leg along the stomach to the heel of the front leg. From the toe of the front leg, pin and sew up to A.

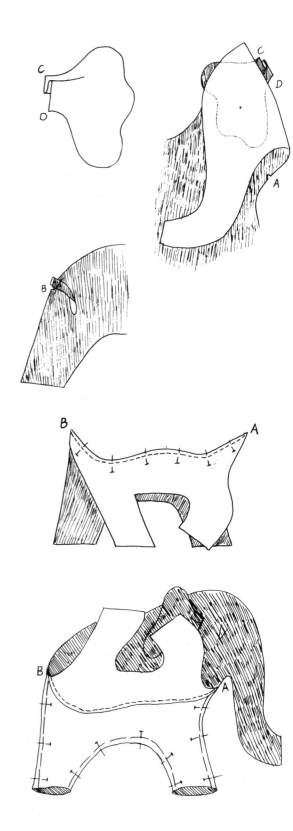

Step 5. Pin, baste, and sew side body #2 to underbody #2, the right sides of the fabric facing, from the toe of the front leg through A and along the bottom of the trunk to the tip. At A, where the four pieces meet, be careful that you do not leave a small gap. Then pin, baste, and sew the upper side of the trunk, over the head, and down the back to the heel of the hind leg. As you sew over the top of the head, be sure an ear isn't accidentally caught into the seam. And just before B see that the base of the tail is sewn into the seam firmly. Pin, baste, and sew the final seam from the toe of the hind leg to the heel of the front leg, leaving an opening of around 4 inches (10 cm) between the legs for turning and stuffing.

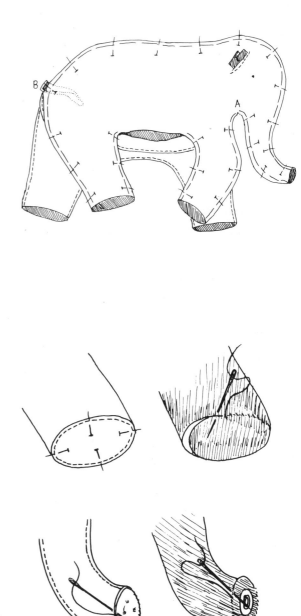

Step 6. There are two methods for sewing on the tip of the trunk and the soles of the feet. If your elephant is made of a fabric that frays easily, it is best to sew them on before you turn it right side out. If you are using a fabric that doesn't fray, you can overcast or blanket-stitch them on after the elephant has been turned right side out.

If you are sewing the soles of the feet in before turning, pin or tack the sole, wrong side of the fabric facing out, at four points, and ease on as you sew. Or you can overcast or blanket-stitch the soles on after the elephant has been turned and stuffed.

If you set the tip of the trunk in before turning, sew the negative snap on the right side of the fabric and pin the tip in, wrong side out, then sew on with tiny overcast stitches.

To sew the tip on after turning and stuffing, sew the negative snap on the tip first and overcast or blanket-stitch the tip on with tiny stitches.

Turning and Stuffing

The elephant should be stuffed very firmly so he will stand properly and have a nicely rounded appearance. When you start stuffing the tip of the trunk and the bottoms of the legs, use walnut-sized pieces of filling and work in larger ones gradually as you stuff the body and neck. Use extra care in stuffing the tops of the legs firmly where they meet the body. These joints are apt to weaken if not very well stuffed.

Finishing

Sew the positive snap to the top of the end of the tail. If the tail is lined, blind-stitch it in place.

If you are not using beads for eyes, you may embroider them with a satin stitch or glue on rounds of felt. But remember that elephants have very tiny eyes. If you prefer to use bead eyes, see page 126.

Betsey Beagle and Her Puppies

Betsey Beagle and her pups are in hound colors of brown, gold, and white. I made three puppies for Betsey, one in white with gold and brown spots to match her, one in gold with white and brown spots, and one in brown with white and gold spots. Each puppy has one foot pad in a different color from the other three. Of course you can ring any changes on the color scheme you wish. Or use a patterned fabric such as a tweed or a mottled plush and omit the spots. I've made this family in white with black spots and thought the result was quite fetching.

I used a wool tweed here, but you can make the beagles in almost any material except one which frays easily since the sewn-on spots have raw edges. I wouldn't use a smooth-finished cotton since Betsey is a large dog, thirty-three inches long, and if she were in smooth cotton, it would take a lot of time and patience in stuffing to keep her from looking lumpy.

Betsey makes a wonderful present for a family since you can make as many puppies as you need for each child to have one for his own. And if you wish to make an elegant gift, she and her puppies look most impressive in a real dog basket.

You will need

- Body fabric for the mother, 40 inches by 48 inches
  (102 cm by 122 cm)
- Body fabric for one puppy, 25 inches by 16 inches
  (64 cm by 41 cm)
- Embroidery thread for eyelids and eyelashes
- 10 positive snaps for the mother and a negative snap for
  each puppy
- Dacron polyester for stuffing, over 2 pounds for the mother
  and three puppies

The Mother Beagle

To draw the patterns, rule lines on wrapping paper across
and down 2 inches apart to make 2-inch by 2-inch squares.
Copy the patterns onto these squares (see page 10).

When you draw these patterns, it is important that the side
body pattern and the underbody pattern match. There is a
very easy way to do this. Draw around the entire outline of
the side body pattern, including the polka-dotted area of the
legs and the stomach. Then draw the curved line at the top
of the polka-dotted area across your pattern.

Before you cut this pattern, place it over another sheet of
paper and cut two identical ones around the outside lines.
Pay no attention to the curved line over the polka-dotted area
at this time.

The paper pattern of the whole beagle without the drawn
curved line over the polka-dotted area is your side body pattern. Then take the paper pattern with the curved line drawn
on it and cut along the curve. Discard the upper portion and
the lower half is your underbody pattern. You then have perfect matches which make sewing the seams much easier and
will produce a well-tailored toy.

Cutting

Lay out the fabric wrong side up and place your patterns on
it, following the directions of the arrows so the nap runs from

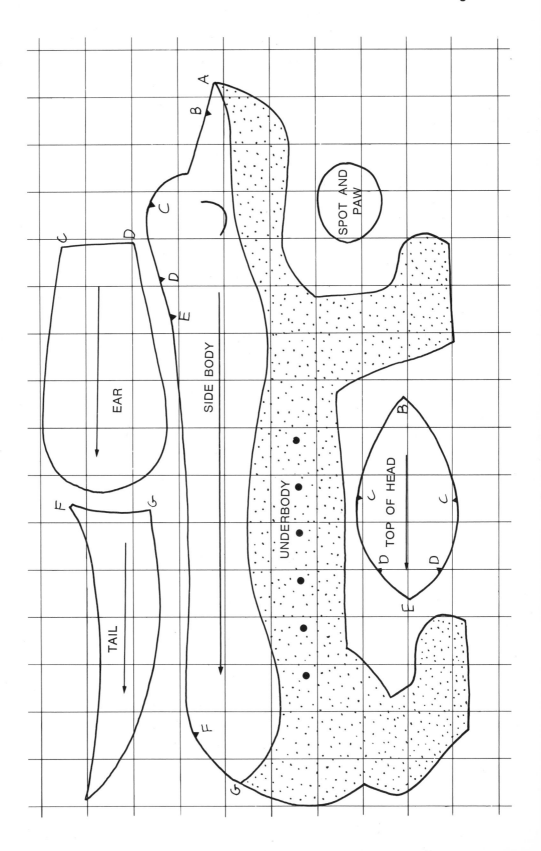

the nose to the tail. Cut 2 side body pieces, flipping the pattern over to reverse it for the second so there will be a right side and a left side. Cut 2 underbodies, reversing one, and 1 top-of-the-head piece and 2 ears, reversing one. Cut two tails, reversing one.

From the contrasting fabrics, cut 2 ears, reversing one, and 5 spots and 4 paw pads.

Mark the As, Bs, etc. Mark the curve of the eyelids with a running stitch in a contrasting colored thread, pulling it through to the right side of the fabric.

Sewing

All seams should be ¼ of an inch (6 mm). Before you start to sew the beagle, it is a good idea to get the smaller pieces sewn and put aside.

Pin and sew the ear pieces together, right sides of the fabrics facing, around the outer edge, leaving the space between C and D open for turning. Clip on the curves and turn.

Pin and sew the two tail pieces together, right sides of the fabric facing, leaving the space between F and G open for turning. Cut across the tip near the seam and turn right side out. Stuff the tail to within ¼ of an inch (6 mm) of the base and close it by basting.

Step 1. Place the spots on the side body pieces, planning both sides at the same time so that they form a pleasing combination when they are put together. The illustration is only a suggestion as I am sure you will want the fun of arranging them yourself.

Baste the spots in place and sew them on around the edges with a zigzag machine stitch in a matching thread or hand-sew them with an invisible hemming stitch or a small blanket stitch.

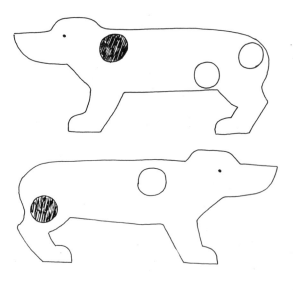

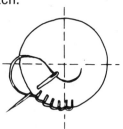

Step 2. Pin, baste, and sew the two underbody pieces together, right sides of the fabric facing, from A to G.

Step 3. Pin and baste the sewn underbody section to one of the side body pieces, right sides of the fabric facing, matching the legs and A at the nose and G at the tail. Then sew from A at the nose down the front of the front leg, leaving the bottom of the paw open. Continue from the back of the front leg up and across the stomach and down to the front of the hind leg again, leaving the bottom of the paw open. Sew up the hind leg to G.

Step 4. Pin, baste, and sew the other side body piece to the other side of the sewn underbody section, right sides of the fabric facing. Repeat as in step 3, leaving the bottoms of the legs open. Also leave an opening of around 5 inches (13 cm) between the legs for turning and stuffing.

Step 5. Pin the inside of the ears face down on the right side of the fabric of the head, matching the Cs and the Ds with ⅛ of an inch (3 mm) of the base of the ears showing from the wrong side, and baste the ears in place.

Step 6. Pin and baste the top of the nose together from A to B. Then pin and baste one side of the top-of-the-head piece to a side body piece, matching the Bs and the Es. Sew from A to E, catching the ear in the seam securely.

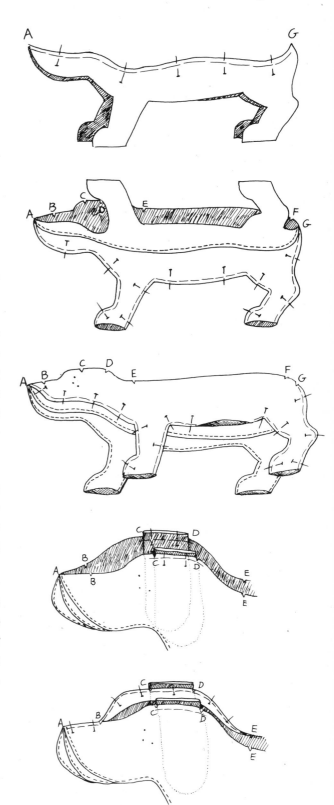

Step 7. Starting at B on the top of the nose, pin and baste the other side of the head piece in place, catching in the ear and continuing from E down the center of the back. Before you reach F, put the tail inside with the Fs and the Gs matching so that the tail will curl up. Baste it in place with ⅛ of an inch (3 mm) of the base showing from the wrong side of the fabric. Then sew from B down the back to G, sewing in the ear and the tail securely as you go.

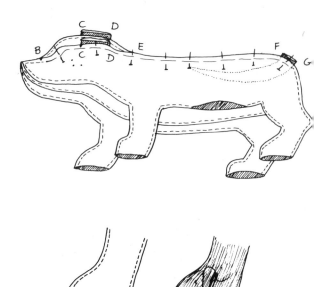

Step 8. There are two ways you can sew in the paw pads.

You can sew them in by machine, first pinning or basting them in place, before you turn the beagle right side out. Or you can turn and stuff her and then sew the pads on with a small overcast stitch.

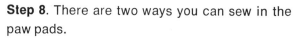

Turning and Stuffing

Clip the curves and check the seams to see if the sewing needs reinforcing anywhere and then turn right side out. As the beagle is not a standing toy, the stuffing should be only moderately firm so she is squeezable. When you stuff the head, shape the forehead, the bridge of the nose, and the nose. The head and the neck should be firmly stuffed so they will keep their shape. Close the opening with small overcast stitches.

Finishing

The eyelids can be done with two rows of stem stitches or one row of chain stitching. The eyelashes are formed by a series of radiating stitches. The best way to make the spacing of the eyelashes even is to do the two at the ends first, then the one in the middle, and then the ones between. Choose a thread or yarn that matches the texture of your fabric.

Sew the positive snaps for her puppies in two rows on the underbody.

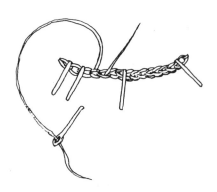

The Beagle Puppies

These are made exactly like the mother except, of course, there are no snaps on the underbody. Instead they have a negative snap just under the nose. One beagle puppy without a snap makes a fine gift by himself.

To draw the puppy patterns, rule lines on wrapping paper across and down 1 inch apart to make 1-inch by 1-inch squares. Copy the patterns onto the squares (see page 10).

Just follow the directions for making the mother beagle, but since the paw pads are so small, you will find it easier to hand-sew them on after the puppy has been stuffed.

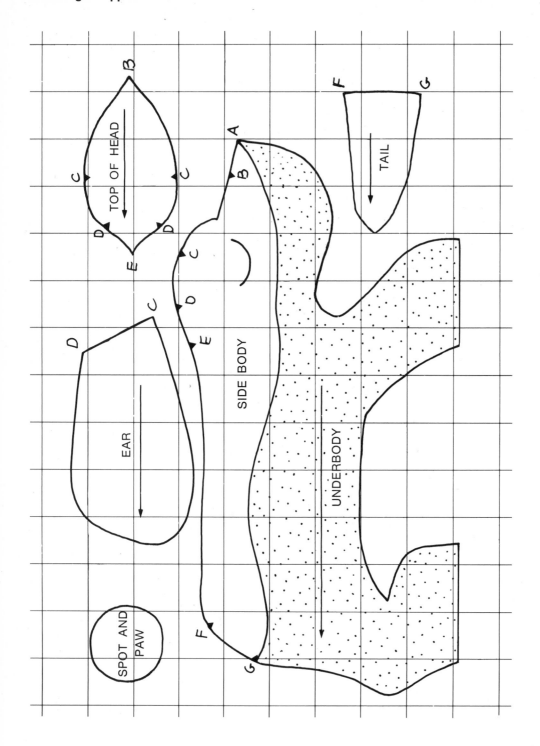

TOP OF HEAD

TAIL

SIDE BODY

UNDERBODY

EAR

SPOT AND PAW

Pretzel People

The pretzel people are contortionists and so limber they can be snapped into knots. You need not make a pair as one by itself can be snapped into all sorts of fantastic positions. And as they are thirty-nine inches tall one alone is an impressive gift. I have found that it is not only children who get a kick out of pretzel people. I've given them to many of my adult friends with happy results.

Choose a fabric such as a knit which has quite a bit of stretch to it. The fabric should be strong since these dolls will be given a lot of active wear. For this pair I chose stretch gabardines in solid green and yellow, so the snaps would show up clearly. With pretzel people you can go wild in your color schemes—real circus colors—and even the faces don't have to be a natural color.

You will need for one doll
- Body fabric, 26 inches by 16 inches (66 cm by 41 cm), of two different colors
- Fabric for face, hands, and feet, 21 inches by 16 inches (53 cm by 41 cm)
- 15 pairs of medium-sized snaps
- Felt for ears, mouth, and eyes, scraps
- Embroidery thread (optional)
- 2 buttons, ⅝ of an inch (16 mm) in diameter, for eyes (optional)
- Knitting wool for a tassel or pompon (optional)
- Dacron polyester for stuffing, 12 ounces

To draw the patterns, rule lines on wrapping paper across and down 1½ inches apart to make 1½-inch by 1½-inch squares. Copy the patterns onto the squares (see page 10).

Cutting
Plan your color scheme and lay out your patterns accordingly. Lay out the fabrics wrong side up with the grain following the arrows on the patterns or at right angles to them. It doesn't matter which way as long as the arms and the legs are cut on the bias. Cut 4 upper body pieces, reversing two by flipping the pattern over. Cut 4 lower body pieces, reversing two, 4 hands, reversing two, and 4 feet, reversing two. Cut 4 head pieces and 4 cap pieces, reversing two.

Cut 2 felt ears. Don't draw the patterns for the ears on the felt as the ears will have raw edges. Just hold the pattern against the felt between the thumb and forefinger and cut around it.

Mark the As, Bs, etc. Pull knotted, contrasting colored thread through to the right sides of the fabric to mark the placing of the eyes.

Sewing
All the seams should be ³⁄₁₆ of an inch (5 mm). If you have a stretch stitch on your machine, use that. If not, use a medium-length stitch.

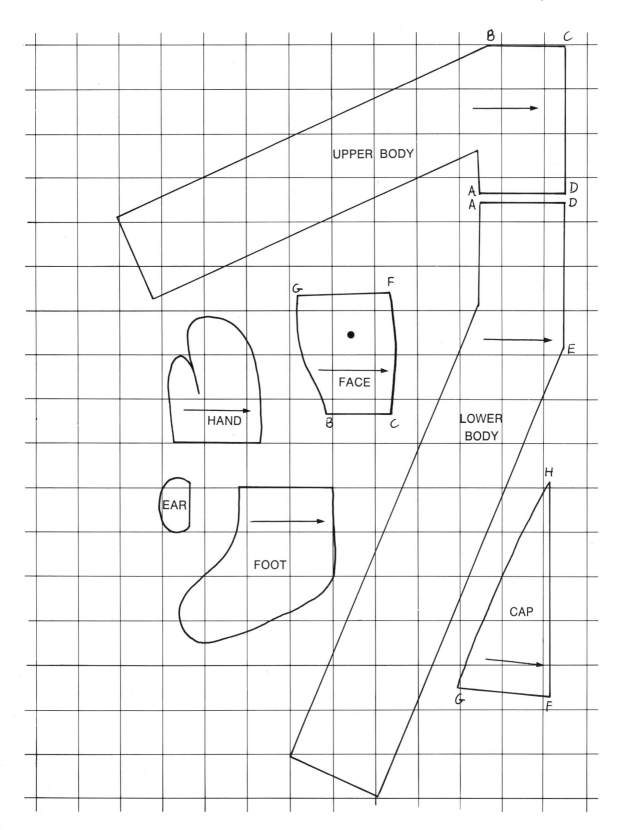

Step 1. Pin and sew the four cap pieces to the four face pieces, matching the Fs and the Gs, with the right sides of the fabrics facing.

Step 2. Pin and sew the neck to the shoulders, matching the Bs and the Cs, right sides of the fabrics facing. Sew the four hands onto the wrists, right sides of the fabrics facing, with the thumbs on the insides.

Step 3. Pin and sew the two upper body halves together, right sides of the fabrics facing, from D to H, matching the seams at C and F carefully.

Step 4. Pin and sew the four feet onto the legs, right sides of the fabrics facing, with the toes pointing out.

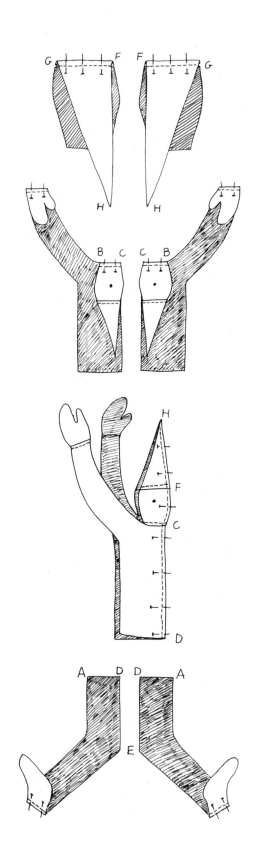

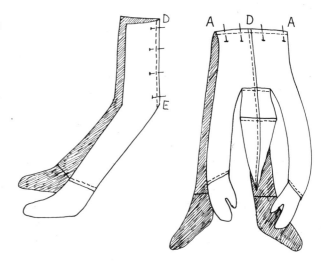

Step 5. Pin and sew the lower body halves together, right sides of the fabrics facing, from D to E.

Step 6. Pin and sew the upper body to the lower body at the waist from A to A, right sides of the fabrics facing. Be very careful to match the seams at D. Repeat with the other side.

Step 7. Place the ears on the face just below G with ⅛ of an inch (3 mm) showing from the wrong side. Pin and baste the two sides together, right sides of the fabrics facing. Be very careful to match the seams at the waist, wrists, ankles, face, and neck. When you sew, stitch the ears in firmly and leave an opening of 3 inches (8 cm) at one side of the waist for turning and stuffing. Leave additional smaller openings on the arms and the legs for easier stuffing.

Turning and Stuffing

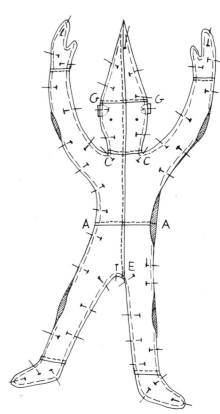

Clip the curves at the neck and under the arms. Cut across the tips of the thumbs and the top of the cap close to the seam. Check all the seams to make sure they are securely sewn, and if they are not, reinforce them by hand. The raw seam edges should be zigzag-stitched by machine or overcast by hand to strengthen them. Remember, this doll will lead a very active life. Turn it right side out and turn the thumbs, toes, and top of the cap completely with the blunt end of a knitting needle.

Because pretzel people are contortionists, they must be stuffed very carefully to keep them flexible. Use very small pieces and stuff medium soft. Stuff the hands and the feet first, and when you have filled the arms and the legs up to the small openings, close them with a small overcast stitch and continue to stuff through the opening at the waist. Make the necks and heads a little firmer than the rest of the doll.

Close the opening at the waist with a small overcast stitch.

Finishing

The snaps can be scattered on the doll at random, alternating positive and negative snaps. If you have made two dolls, you can place the snaps on the second in a mirror image of the first so they can dance and perform acrobatics together. You can plan your own placing of the snaps or you may follow the scheme in these drawings.

Sew on buttons for the eyes (see page 126) or use rounds of felt which you can glue or sew on. You can, if you wish, sew a series of straight stitches for eyelashes. The best way to make the spacing and angles of the eyelashes even is to do the end ones first, then the middle ones, and then the ones in between.

I used a curve of bright pink felt for the mouths and glued it on. You can experiment with different curves until you find one you like. Or you might prefer to stem-stitch the mouth instead.

If you like, you can finish off the top of the pointed cap with a tassel or a pompon.

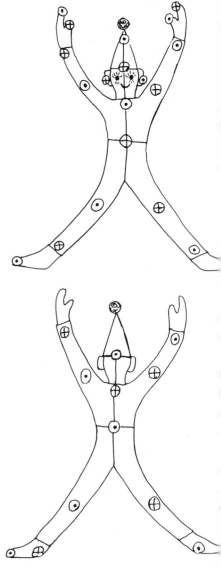

Octopus

This octopus has more than meets the eye in the photograph. Not only is he affectionate-looking and huggable, but with Velcro fasteners sewn to the underside of the tentacles, he can hug back. You can wear him like a boa or he can weave his tentacles around each other in an endless variety of positions.

I made the outer body of this one in a light yellow, brushed-lamb fabric. He really is best in a pile fabric or a woolly one as he is a large (two feet and seven inches long) and cuddly creature. The tentacle linings and the underbody should be a flat fabric so the Velcro fasteners or the snaps are not lost in the pile. I used a printed cotton with a lemon yellow background, but he can be made into a dressier octopus with rich-colored-silk tentacle linings and underbody.

He does involve a lot of sewing, but he is quite easy to put together. The only tricky part is sewing in the inner mouth, which is not hard to do but is hard to explain, so follow the instructions slowly, *always* work with the right sides of the fabrics facing, and pin it into place before you sew.

This is one of my favorite toys and I hope you will have fun making him.

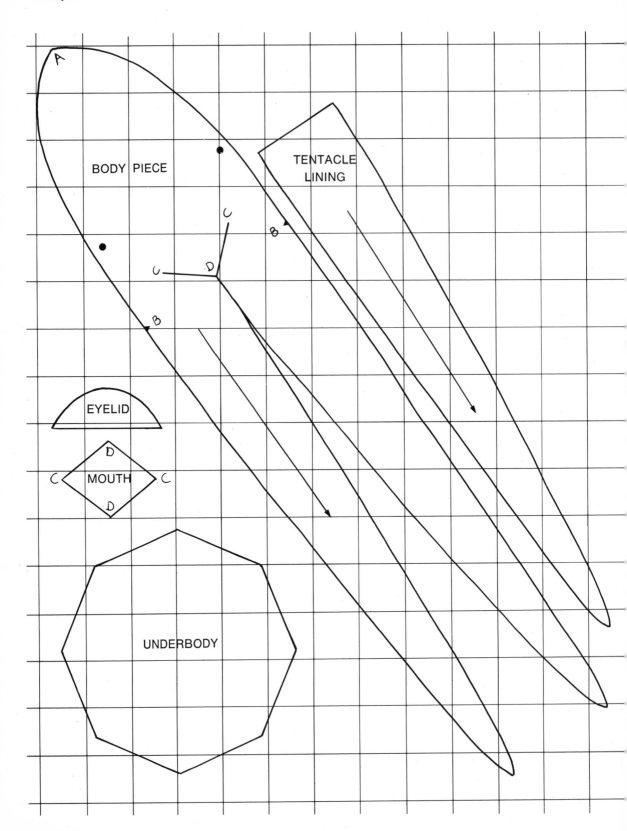

You will need

Fur fabric for the body, 40 inches by 36 inches
(102 cm by 91 cm)
Printed cotton for the underbody and the tentacle linings,
1 yard (91 cm)
24 pairs of Velcro fasteners, ¾ of an inch (19 mm) in
diameter or large snaps
Felt or velveteen for the inside of the mouth, a scrap
(optional as the printed cotton can be used)
2 round buttons for eyes, approximately 1½ inches
(38 mm) in diameter (optional as soft fabric eyes are very
effective on the octopus)
Dacron polyester for stuffing, 2 pounds

To draw the patterns, rule lines on wrapping paper across and
down 2 inches apart to make 2-inch by 2-inch squares. Copy
the pattern onto these squares (see page 10).

Cutting

Lay out the fur fabric wrong side up. Place your patterns on
it, following the directions of the arrows so the nap runs from
the top of the head to the tip of the tentacles. Cut 4 body
pieces and 2 eyelids. Mark the face on only one body piece.
Draw the lines between D and the Cs to form the mouth and
mark the eyes by pulling a knotted, contrasting colored thread
through to the right side of the fabric.

Lay out the cotton print, following the arrows for the grain
of the fabric or the direction of the pattern. Cut 8 tentacle linings and 1 underbody. Cut 1 inside of the mouth if you are
using the print, otherwise cut 1 inside of the mouth of felt or
velveteen.

Sewing

All seams should be ¼ of an inch (6 mm).

Step 1. Pin, baste, and sew the body piece with
the face markings to another body piece, right
sides of the fabric facing, from A to B. Then pin,
baste, and sew the other two body pieces
together in the same way.

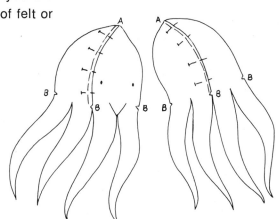

Step 2. To put the two halves of the head together, pin and baste from B over the top of the head at A, matching the As exactly. Just past A leave a 4-inch (10-cm) opening for turning and stuffing. Continue pinning and basting to B on the other side. Then sew.

Step 3. Pin and sew the eight cotton tentacle linings to the underbody piece, right sides of the fabric facing.

Step 4. Lay the underbody and the tentacle linings on the fur fabric head and tentacles, right sides of the fabrics facing. Match the bases of the tentacles and pin and baste up and down the tentacles so the tips match. Sew a seam from the base of a tentacle to the tip and then back up the other side to the base. Continue down the next tentacle until all eight are sewn.

Step 5. To sew in the inside of the mouth, cut lines from D to the two Cs. This will form a V-shaped flap. Turn the flap up and pin and baste the diamond-shaped mouth piece, right sides of the fabrics facing, from D at the top point of the flap to the Cs at each side. From the Cs, continue pinning and basting, right sides of the fabrics facing, down to where the bases of the tentacles meet. Then sew in place.

Turning and Stuffing

Before turning, clip the curves on the top of the head and the angles between the tentacles. Cut straight across, close to the seams, at the tips of the tentacles and the tip of the mouth flap. Then check the seams to see if there are any places that need reinforcing by hand.

Turn the octopus right side out and stuff. The tentacles should not be stuffed too firmly as the octopus is much more fun to play with if they are flexible. Close the opening with small, firm overcast stitches and brush the fur fabric gently at the seams to free any fur that may have been caught in them.

Finishing

Place three pairs of Velcro fasteners down the middle of the tentacle linings, alternating the looped and hooked fasteners, and sew them down. If you are using snaps, sew them on, alternating the positive and the negative snaps.

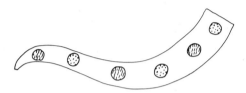

If you are using fabric eyes (see page 124), make them from circles 3 inches (8 cm) in diameter and add pupils 1¼ of an inch (32 mm) in diameter. I placed the pupils so as to give him a shy, demure expression.

If you are using button eyes, see page 126.

After the eyes are sewn on, pin the eyelids in place. The bottom of the lid should be parallel to the slant of the mouth on the opposite side. Sew them on with a hemming stitch around the upper curve.

Finishing the Features

Eyes

Placing the eyes correctly is tremendously important since this is what gives the animal his expression. Use the thread marks as a guide but if, after the toy is stuffed, for any reason they don't please you, follow your instincts and change the position of the eyes. And if by any chance the thread marks don't come out even, choose the one you like best and match the other eye to it.

Soft Fabric Eyes

Step 1. Cut two identical circles of the fabric. With a strong thread, do a running stitch around the outer edge to form a drawstring.

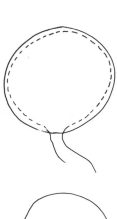

Step 2. Pull up gently and then stuff to the fullness you wish.

Step 3. Tuck the opening underneath, pin in place, and hem on with small stitches.

Step 4. Cut a smaller circle of felt for the pupil, pin in place, and sew on with small stitches or glue it on.

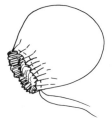

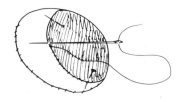

Padded Felt Eyes

Cut two identical circles of felt. If you are going to have pupils, you can use white felt and cut two smaller circles of dark felt. Or if you do not wish pupils, you can use dark felt for the eyes.

Sew the pupil on the eye with small hemming stitches. Then pin the eye in place and sew it three-quarters of the way around. Then tuck in a little piece of stuffing and complete the sewing.

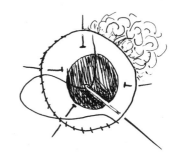

Pupils

It is fun to experiment with placing the pupils on the felt or soft fabric eyes to achieve the expression you like best for the animal or doll. Pin the pupil on the eye in different positions until you find the right one. Then sew it on.

Bead or Button Eyes for Small Animals

Step 1. Tie a small knot in buttonhole thread and, using a long needle, pull the thread through from one side of the head to the other at the eye marks.

Step 2. Thread a bead or a button on the needle and go back through the head, coming out on the far side as close to the small knot as you can.

Step 3. Repeat step 2 with the second button or bead and then go back to the first, securing it again. Continue this process several times until the beads or buttons are securely sewn. Pull the beads or buttons tight each time you sew through the head. Finish by making several small stitches as close as you can to the center of the button or bead.

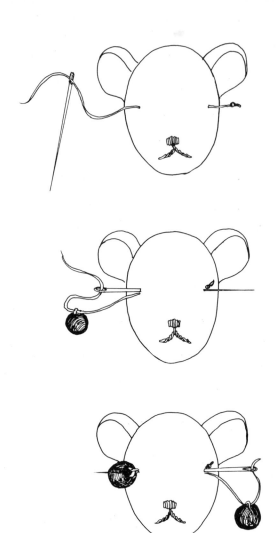

Whiskers

Whiskers add lovely finishing touches to small furry animals as well as some of the larger ones. Match the size of the thread to the size of the animal. A regular 50 sewing thread is fine for small animals. A button thread is good for the larger ones. And on some an 8-pound fishing line is effective. The whiskers shouldn't contrast too much in color unless you wish a bold, fantastic effect.

To Make Whiskers

Use a long needle and a fairly long thread. The whiskers should go on the animal's upper lip below and slightly back of the nose. Put the needle where you want the first whisker and pull it out on the other side of the nose, leaving a long whisker sticking out from the first side of the nose. Then put the needle back into the nose as close as you can to where it came out. Pull the needle through again but this time pull it tight. This second stitch is a stay stitch and will secure the whiskers. Go back again and sew another tiny stay stitch on the other side.

Then go back and forth, alternately making long loops and stay stitches. Plan the placement of each loop before you pull the needle through so they are spaced well. Make the loops much longer than you need them. Then when the whiskers are finished, trim them to the length you wish.

Stitches for Noses and Mouths

Satin Stitch

This is a good stitch for noses. Use single-strand glossy embroidery thread. Start at the center of the nose with the longest stitch and then work a slightly shorter second stitch on one side. Continue with parallel stitches of decreasing length. Don't pull the threads too tight and always insert the needle into the fabric at the top and pull it out below. When half the nose is completed, do a matching half on the other side of the center stitch.

Stem Stitch

To stem-stitch a mouth, bring the needle out just under the nose and push it in again about ¼ of an inch (6 mm) farther along the line on which you are working. Bring the needle out again close beside and halfway along the first stitch. Always keep the needle pointing toward the row of stitches being formed and bring the needle out halfway along the stitch just formed. Make the stitches very even and do not pull them too tight.

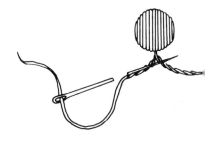

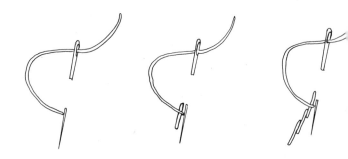